THE THIRD HOUSE OF CONGRESS

JOHN KNOX

authorHOUSE®

AuthorHouse™
1663 Liberty Drive
Bloomington, IN 47403
www.authorhouse.com
Phone: 1 (800) 839-8640

Published by AuthorHouse 03/13/2017

ISBN: 978-1-5246-7568-4 (sc)
ISBN: 978-1-5246-7566-0 (hc)
ISBN: 978-1-5246-7567-7 (e)

Library of Congress Control Number: 2017903696

Print information available on the last page.

INTRODUCTION

The Third House of Congress is intended to serve as a charter for the movement to promote and enact the idea it contains.

INDICATIONS

We all know our government is off the rails. The instruments of self-governing we have inherited are not controlling the institutions we have inherited. We see indications of it daily. This condition undermines our ability to meet the challenges of this century. Each day we miss opportunities.

1. Government policy is rarely wise and up to date.
2. The two parties serve party interest before the interests of the country.
3. Campaigns are a circus.
4. Money influences every debate.
5. The Supreme Court infringes on the Legislative Branch.
6. The President infringes on the Legislative Branch
7. The Senate fails at oversight.
8. The House fails to control the purse strings.
9. Our wealth is squandered even as nothing gets done.
10. Business flees this environment.
11. Reform efforts fail to address the systemic causes.
12. Every day opportunities are missed and real people are hurt

Our form of government is sound. The remedy must not fundamentally alter our form of government, nor should it depart from the spirit in which it was founded.

THE CONSTITUTIONAL AMENDMENT

The Third House Amendment will establish and empower a Third House of United States Congress. But unlike the House and the Senate, the Third House of Congress will contain no politicians. The Third House is the Ordinary American House. Instead of campaigns favoring the party comrades, the wealthy, the cunning and charismatic, the Third House will be filled by Random Lot.

With this amendment we can send ordinary Americans to guard our interests in Washington. These Americans will be invested with an authority that enables them to slow down or stop federal legislation, to investigate any part of the government, and to take remedial action against waste, fraud, and corruption.

Think of this amendment as your reset button on the government.

Amendment XXVIII . . .

1. The Congress of the United States shall consist of Three Houses: The Senate; The House of Representatives; and The Assembly of United States Tribunes.

2. The Assembly of United States Tribunes shall be comprised of one Tribune from each state: to serve a term of one year only; each Tribune shall have one vote.

3. No person shall be Tribune who has not been five years a citizen of the United States and five years a resident of the state that they have been appointed to represent.

4. Each office of Tribune shall be filled using a two step process: the first step shall be a random drawing or a regular rotation, which shall determine the county, parish, independent city, or geographical division from which the Tribune shall be chosen; the second step shall be a random drawing to appoint the Tribune (the person chosen by the drawing may refuse service or designate an alternate to serve in their stead). The appointment process shall be held by the states, shall be completed not less than one year prior to vacancies, and shall be repeated until the appointment is accepted.

5. Each Tribune shall be subject to recall at any time by state referendum. The Tribune may be impeached by the legislature of the state that they are representing for any criminal indictment occurring while the Tribune is in office.

6. The Assembly may alter the starting and ending times of the terms of any part of the whole Assembly by unanimous vote, providing that no Tribune is enabled to serve for more than one year as a result.

7. If vacancies happen, by resignation or otherwise, the chosen successor to that office may serve, pro tempore, until the new term begins, through which they may serve as usual. If the successor is not available, the executive of the state may make temporary appointments.

8. The Assembly shall appoint a chief fiduciary officer who shall serve during good behavior, who shall be responsible for the correct and effective performance of the Assembly and who shall be accountable for any failures thereof. The Assembly shall elect a presiding Tribune and form committees as needed; but no authority shall be invested by internal organizational resolutions.

9. The Assembly shall be a full and coequal House of United States Congress; shall be invested with all duties, powers and immunities common to the Senate and the House of Representatives (except those listed herein); and each Tribune shall receive equal compensation, which shall to be paid out of the United States Treasury.

10. The Assembly shall not be privileged to secret matters of national security.

11. Every article of legislation approved by the Assembly is entitled to a timely vote by the United States Senate and the House of Representatives.

12. Every article requiring the concurrence of congress shall be sent to the Assembly; any part approved by the Assembly may proceed and be made final; any part not approved by the Assembly shall be returned, together with objections, to the house in which it originated, who shall proceed to reconsider it. If after such reconsiderations two-thirds of that house vote to affirm, than it shall be sent, together with objections, to the other house to be reconsidered. If two-thirds of that house vote to affirm then the article may proceed and be made final. If the Assembly makes no returns or objections within ten days of receipt (excepting Sundays) the article may proceed and be made final. Any article having previously received two-thirds approving vote in both the Senate and the House of Representatives is exempt from this section.

13. The Assembly is empowered to form commissions to investigate any United States government agency, official or employee for unconstitutional, unlawful, or unethical acts of public authority, and for incompetent performance of duties. The Assembly is empowered to investigate private persons and organizations who receive monies from the United States government (or otherwise

act on behalf of United States Government agencies, officials or employees) for unconstitutional, unlawful, or unethical actions, and for incomplete or incompetent fulfillment of material obligations. Upon two-thirds resolution the Assembly may compel the reform of any United States government agency that is not specifically established by the constitution of the United States, impeach any United States government official who has not been elected by the people, compel the Senate to hear articles of impeachment against persons holding elected office in the United States government; or suspend United States contractual agreements with any private person or organization pending congressional action.

The structure, functions, and powers created by this amendment will restore an appropriate measure of control over the domestic policies of our government. This amendment will enable our people to better resist unwanted policies, and assist in initiating more favorable policies now and in the future. It will help us to put right some of the policies that have already been enacted.

Part I

THE REMEDY

What would you do as Tribune?

Individuals who are prepared to support a new representative institution in their government should understand its operations. This part describes the essential aspects of our cause.

> (Paragraph 1) "The Congress of the United States shall consist of three houses: the Senate; the House of Representatives; and the Assembly of United States Tribunes."

The Assembly provides a different type of representation. It is constituted to reflect the diverse walks of life in America. The Senate and the House of Representatives are filled by high-stakes popular elections. Membership in these bodies is limited to men and women who are suitable to win elections—a small and distinct fraction of the American population. A Tribune, on the other hand, could be almost anyone.

The Tribunes will be ordinary Americans, diverse in nature and experience. They will not be bound to any interest by elections. Rather, they have been called forth in the spirit of civic responsibility, and have accepted the call. Their purpose at the Capitol is to defend their locality, their state, and their walk of life. Their purpose is to defend everything that they know, and to defend what they may not know on behalf of those who do.

With such a character the Assembly will bear little resemblance to the ultra elite Senate or the ideological battleground that is the House of Representatives. This is a good thing; such distinctions are the life-blood of any system of checks and balances.

The purpose and the duty of the Assembly is to guard against the costly and ill-conceived legislation we have come to expect out of the House and Senate. The Assembly is designed to be an almost seamless extension of the American nation. The Assembly will sit near to Washington, be first to respond to every act of government, be first to sound the alarm, and be the first to mount a resistance.

The authority of the Tribunes will be the greatest asset in efforts to reform public policy and restore the promise of our system. The Assembly and its relationship to the people may be able to replace hundreds of thousands of unelected decision makers: I mean those of our countrymen who earn their keep regulating the rest of us and who are part cause and part symptom of the dysfunction that we are trying to overcome.

Our political system sorely needs the perspective of ordinary Americans. The Assembly will become a vital part of the American system.

> (Paragraph 2) "The Assembly of United States Tribunes shall be comprised of one Tribune from each state: to serve one term of one year only; each Tribune shall have one vote."

The individual appointed by lot is given the opportunity to serve for one year in the United States Congress. Fifty such individuals will be part of the legislative process each year. Every resource and expertise will be at his or her disposal. They will represent the people of their state, their county, and their walk of life: their local interests. They will work with elected leaders, private parties, and one another to improve the policies that come out of Washington. The fifty Americans will participate in the process with a careful eye on domestic policy. Their prestigious station and imminent return to private life will promote urgency and good faith in all that they do.

The Assembly is comprised of only fifty Tribunes because of the role it is intended to play in the Congress. The powers invested in the Assembly are not decisive. The Tribunes are not lawmakers and the Assembly is not framing policy. Its role is oversight. Oversight must be pursued with single-minded determination. Larger bodies of people are not as effective. Their members develop a sense of anonymity. They become more confrontational, while at the same time more willing to compromise. The work of the Assembly would suffer as a result. The Assembly is designed for the job at hand. It will function best having only fifty members.

One Tribune from each state will be more effective than multiple Tribunes from each state. We want each Tribune to bear one hundred percent of the responsibility to the state that appoints them. We do not want any situation where one person will defer to another or become embroiled in a debate over the issue. We want the Tribune to go in to each vote without any peripheral concerns. The Tribunes are ordinary people who are appointed to serve a role in our legislative process. Every factor must serve to improve their capacity to fill that role. That means consolidating all authority, responsibility, and visibility in one person. That means removing every potential excuse. This is what makes a person the best that they can be.

This is the ideal Tribune: an ordinary person, even of humble talent, but who is inspired to the highest possible standard. That is what we will design our Assemblyhouse to promote. That is what we will instill in our personnel. That is the reason for the short one-year terms. And that is the reason for the single office of Tribune from each state, to inspire each ordinary American to be the best that they can possibly be. That is who we want overseeing our legislature.

The short one-year terms will result in a great variety of Americans serving in the Assembly. In just twenty years, one thousand individuals will have served in the Third House, roughly the same number as will have served during the same period in the Senate and the House of Representatives combined. Over the course of one hundred years about twice as many Americans will have served as Tribune as will have served as Senators and Representatives combined. This will add a dimension of variety to representation in the United States government.

The fifty Americans will also be distinct in the fact that they, of all of the congress, did not seek the office that they have agreed to fulfill. They are real people, who led conventional lives, until one day they were called to serve. When called they put down what they were doing and agreed to serve for one year only. This is as close to the 'reluctant leader' ethos of the founding era as we are going to get.

A single American appointed by lot and made Tribune for one year is at least as valid an instrument of self-governing as a Senator or Representative.

(Sidebar; Fifty Only)

Even with only fifty members the two-step appointment process and the short, one-year, terms will ensure that a wide variety of backgrounds will be present. Input from the public will always be welcomed, and each Tribune will have access to a staff of professionals for assistance. The Assembly will be able to fill its role effectively comprised of just fifty Americans.

(Sidebar: Restoring Trust)

The Assembly is essentially a jury: the most credible and least corruptible body in the American experience. As such, the Tribunes will enjoy a unique station of trust among the American people. No pundit, newsman, or politician has the audience or the respect that the official resolutions of the Assembly will receive. This situation will not be wasted. The Assembly will constantly disseminate facts and real-world information on the tough issues. This greater and broader respect will ease the way for controversial reforms. Just one party of trust will make it possible to overcome the suspicions and controversy that has tied up our government for generations. Bold reforms like we have not seen in fifty years may be possible.

> (Paragraph 3.) "No person shall be Tribune who has not been five years a citizen of the United States and five years a resident of the state that they have been appointed to represent."

This paragraph establishes only the most basic qualifications to be Tribune. The laws of each state can determine further qualifications. Nothing in this amendment will prevent the states from imposing further qualifications, such as longer residence in the state, or a ban on service by convicted felons. The Tribunes serve under state law, and state law shall determine the qualifications for service as Tribune.

The qualifications for service in the Third House will be maintained in the same manner as voting rights. They will be the prerogative of the states; but they will be limited by the equal protection clause of the Fourteenth Amendment. State law will determine from what pool the lots shall be drawn: all citizens eligible under this paragraph, only eligible voters, only registered voters, only the jury pool, or some other civic distinction. The states are thus permitted to establish the standards that they see fit. But the qualifications will be subject to the same long-standing tradition of judicial oversight as our voting rights.

> (Paragraph 4.) "Each office of Tribune shall be filled using a two-step process of drawing lots."

The purpose of representation is to guarantee a responsible, responsive, and accountable government. Anyone who is watching can see that the Senate and the House are neither responsive nor accountable. The government has accumulated too much baggage and the stakes are too high for the prospect of elections to affect the politicians as it was intended to.

The power of the vote is not likely to return. This is a function of the baggage and high-stakes present in the conditions of today. Domestic policy is what has changed. Domestic policy is where most of the baggage and high-stakes reside.

When our government was launched it had no domestic policy. There was no such thing as a domestic policy in the federal government. The federal government was designed and established to conduct our outward-looking affairs. Its powers were enumerated in the constitution. It was established to set uniform trade and immigration policies, conduct diplomacy, and secure a national defense. The representative bodies that it was given were designed for these tasks, not to enact or maintain a comprehensive domestic policy. The role of the government informed the construction of its representative offices. The role of the government is the reason representation was set up as it was. But today the role of the government has been increased. Under the auspices of domestic policy, that same government moves enormous sums of money around the country. It has multiplied its duties. It has enacted millions of laws and regulations. It has grown its unelected bodies and bindings beyond anything that it was established to do. And, after all of this growth, the only parts of the government that are responsible to the people in elections are the same distant and elite Senate and House of Representatives that were designed and established back when it managed only outward-looking affairs.

The Senate and the House of Representatives are too distant and too isolated to effectively manage a domestic policy on the scope it exists today. This problem is manifest. Many Americans do not realize how poorly constructed our domestic policy is. Or they have decided that it is tolerable as it is. But many are writhing beneath its effects. Many others see it as it is and would prefer to begin its improvement.

The Third House is the only remedy designed in this century, under the present conditions, to restore a balance that has been lost. This amendment will ultimately lead to much better governing. The Third House Amendment brings representation back down to Earth. It gives us a full and coequal House of Congress to balance out the inimical characteristics shared by the other two houses, due to their reliance on electoral politics.

Representation by random lot is not prey to any of the problems arising from campaigns. No money can change hands. No party controls the purse strings. Class warfare and division are not factors. No pundits or special interests can intimidate or apply pressure to a Tribune. The Tribunes are not forced to side with anyone; they can vote their conscience in every instance.

The Third House will not be just another excuse-factory: this institution will function. It will serve as a balance to mitigate the tendencies of the Senate and the House of Representatives. The advent of representation by random lot will add impetus to the congressional functions, even as it moderates their excesses.

> (Paragraph 4 Cont.) "... the first step shall be a random drawing or a regular rotation, which shall determine the county, parish, independent city, or geographical division from which the Tribune shall be chosen ... The second step shall appoint the Tribune."

The first step is essential to this remedy. By first choosing the locality from which to appoint the Tribune we establish a remedy to compensate for an imbalance in our system of representation: the tendency of electoral politics to favor the common interests at the expense of the particular interests. (Part II of this book is dedicated to the examination of this factor.) The greatest scope of particular interests that are relevant to governing is still determined by geographical location. By deciding the locality in a separate step we guarantee that every region will be represented equally, and without regard to population density.

The first house of legislature—the Senate—represents states' rights. The second house of legislature—the House of Representatives—represents the populations of each state equally by their numbers. The Third House of Congress will represent our diverse walks of life, our particular interests. That means our trades and professions, the interests of our geographical region. The Third House will safeguard the interests that are not common to every American and is therefore at a disadvantage in any elected body. This form of representation is long overdue.

The process of appointment by random selection enables the Tribunes to side with the smallest and least represented interests. The geographical component to the appointment process improves this effect by helping to assure that the individuals serving as Tribune will periodically have been drawn from the most diverse regions and walks of life. The Tribunes, each in their turn, will come to serve from a community with a background and an agenda. When a Tribune is appointed from a sparsely populated rural county, the interests in the region, or in similar regions, will enjoy a period of representation unlike any they would ever have in the US House of Senate.

The Third House of Congress is designed for a specific purpose. It is a remedy to an existing imbalance. This remedy pays no respect to the numbers within the respective counties. The Tribunes are not elected and they are not lawmakers. The Tribunes are Defenders of the People. The number of inhabitants living in the county from which they are drawn is not relevant to their purpose.

A Word On The County Lines

County Government, and the geographical delimitations of the counties, usually pre-date the state government to which they are now subject. In almost every locale around this country, the counties were the first form of government jurisdiction. The counties formed the states, just as the states formed the federal government. It is often said that the states are the foundation of the American system. If that were so, then one would have to reckon the counties to be the bedrock that lies beneath the foundation.

The lines delineating the counties represent certain factors, immutable to our system of representative government. These lines were decided as the government was first taking shape. The counties are our native, organic form of representative government. They are actually one of the most significant legacies given to us by our history. And they are extremely valuable in restoring the true spirit of our system.

In the inhabited regions, the county lines were established voluntarily back before the advent of state government, which was back before the supremacy of politics in every project. The county lines were informed by practical purposes. No other geographical lines are as closely tied to practical purposes.

The lines of our counties were informed by two specific rules, both of which were practical necessities. The first rule was distance, from the days of foot travel and horseback. Back east the county lines were drawn to establish a geographical jurisdiction with no point more than a day's walk from the county seat, which was approximately twenty miles. Out west the standard was usually set at one day's ride; about forty miles.

The other rule was to enclose a cohesive community of interest within the jurisdiction of the government that the people would have to share. This was back before the government could simply force itself on every person and community. It was important that the body that was setting the common rules would bind only those folks who, in general, would benefit from the same type of rules. For example, farmers and ranchers needed different land use and commerce policies. It was a simple thing for a government representing a predominance of ranchers to thoughtlessly (or maliciously) enact rules that would wind up bankrupting the minority population of farmers. This actually happened out west, as did the reverse. Innumerable other examples can be given as well. Loggers, miners, and trappers all had different policy needs. The cities and the rural areas have different governing needs that frame our debates even today. This subject is examined further in Part II.

In the days before state government, the exercise of force on behalf of rules was a dubious prospect. It was vital that the rules made by the organizations of government only bind together, as far as possible, a community of shared or non-conflicting interests. And so, the county lines were drawn specifically to enclose only communities of shared or non-conflicting interests. This was common wisdom before force took its place.

Retaining a coherent set of interests within the jurisdiction of each county was accomplished by first observing topographical realities that influenced the interests of the people. Ridgelines and river-fords hindered travel and shipment of goods. Marshes were all but impassable. The economic effects of the topography itself were influential. A lush river valley would favor farming, while a timbered hill country would be populated by loggers. Dusty plains served only pastoral enterprises. We see these features are where the county lines stand to this day.

The lines of most counties were essentially determined by economic concerns. The County Fair was more of a clearinghouse for the goods produced by the county, than the Galas that they have become in the last century. Economics were never the only factor, only the most common. County lines were also established to encompass communities of certain religious denominations so that they might make rules that suited their particular inclinations. We can certainly see the legacy of this practice in many places to this day. This is the way things were formerly done in America: community integrity was a very intentional aspect of the American System.

But the county lines are not as relevant as they once were. Our communities are dislocated and shuffled together; agriculture and resource gathering are not as great a proportion of the economy as they once were; we can travel much farther and with greater ease; the state and federal government totally dominate governing in every place. The counties are easily forgotten.

The counties are not irrelevant. The county lines are essential in that they capture the very essence of representative government, as brought into existence by the USA. The counties are the foundational form of government in America. They will always be relevant for that reason. But they are also relevant because they are sized and configured to serve a single community of interest. And while the community within each county is not as coherent as it once was, the proximity still determines the overwhelming scope of interest. If the current period of dislocation and flux ever eases—which the Third House movement may help to remedy—the communities of interest may become more cohesive yet again.

The geographical delimitations of the counties are the best feasible manner of representing the particular interests of the USA. They are ready made districts from which to choose our Tribunes.

> (Paragraph 5.) "Each Tribune shall be subject to recall at any time by state referendum . . ."

The voters of the state may recall the Tribune of their state at any time. It is unlikely that such a step will be taken during the short, one-year term. However, the power to recall officials is, or should be, a right of We the People, in all cases. The government is too big, too active, and too unstoppable to not be subject to recall.

> (Paragraph 5, cont.) ". . . or the Tribune may be impeached by the legislature of the state they are representing for any criminal indictment occurring while the Tribune is in office."

A recall effort is an extraordinary undertaking. Therefore, in cases of bad behavior, the legislature of the state may remove the Tribune from office by impeachment proceedings.

In the future, the state and federal government will enact laws prohibiting the Tribunes from taking gifts. The Tribunes have no elections; they will not be permitted to receive anything of value. If they are found to have received anything of value, or to have agreed to receive anything of value, they will be subject to indictment under federal or state law.

Paragraph five of this amendment permits the legislature of the state to act immediately to remove the Tribune from office in such a case. The removal does not have to wait for a conviction in the criminal proceeding, but may be enacted immediately upon indictment.

> (Paragraph 6.) "The Assembly may alter the starting and ending times of the terms of any part of the whole Assembly, by unanimous vote, provided that no Tribune is enabled to serve more than one year as a consequence."

This paragraph enables the Assembly to stagger the terms of its offices. For example, the Charter Service (Part IV) will initiate the terms of office so that half of the Tribunes vacate office every six months. This is to provide more continuity to the Assembly than if all the Tribunes retired at once. This paragraph enables the practice to be amended as the wisdom of each generation succeeds the last.

> (Paragraph 7.) "If vacancies happen, by resignation or otherwise, the chosen successor to that office may serve, pro tempore, until the new term begins, through which they may serve as usual. If the successor is not available, the executive of the state may make temporary appointments."

A Tribune appointed in the usual manner will fill vacancies, without delay. If this is impossible, the office will be filled temporarily in the same manner prescribed for the other congressional offices.

> (Paragraph 8.) "The Assembly shall appoint a Chief Fiduciary Officer, who shall serve during good behavior, and who shall be responsible for the correct and effective performance of the Assembly and accountable for any failures thereof."

The Chief Fiduciary Officer is responsible for the workings of the Assemblyhouse. The duties of this office are to make certain that the Tribunes have, at their disposal, every resource and expertise needed to accomplish and promote their work.

This office is essentially a management and executive position: Chief of Staff. As such, this office has no vote and no authority in the workings of the Assembly. However, the Chief could not be simply an employee of the Assemblyhouse, nor of the federal government. With the terms of the Tribunes being only one year, it is necessary to establish an officer to provide continuity, to oversee, and to be responsible, for the whole operation. It was further necessary to establish an office with the authority and responsibility to make fiduciary decisions for the business of the Assembly and in promoting the work of each Tribune, when needed, after the term of the Tribune has ended.

For these reasons it was necessary to charter this office in the amendment itself.

> (Paragraph 8 cont.) ". . . The Assembly shall elect a presiding Tribune and form committees as needed; but no authority shall be invested by internal organizational resolutions."

The presiding Tribune will naturally be the speaker of this house. Organizing business, observing protocols and calling votes are among the duties of this position. Committees shall be formed to undertake projects, oversee investigations, and hear the concerns of the people. But none of these stations shall be conferred with any authority greater than that retained by each member of the Assembly.

By this charter each Tribune retains the right to equal status in the Assembly. Any member may call to order the Assembly, to present evidence, or call for a vote. The pernicious tricks of the committee system will not be permitted to take root in the Third House of Congress.

> (Paragraph 9.) "The Assembly shall be a full and coequal house of United States Congress; shall be invested with all duties, powers and immunities common to the Senate and the House of Representatives (except those listed herein); and each Tribune shall receive equal compensation, to be paid out of the United States Treasury."

The Third House of Congress shall take its place in the framework of the Constitution. The Assembly will retain all of the autonomy in its own affairs, as the other two houses retain in theirs, as is secured to them by article one, section 4, 5 and 6 of the United States Constitution.

The Assembly will convene and adjourn on schedule with the Congress (but the Tribunes will work throughout the year)

Every institution develops a character of its own. Even with the terms limited to one year, the Assembly will develop a culture of its own and take on certain reliable characteristics. Most of these will result from the sections and clauses in this amendment. A few will be derived from the protocols adopted by the early leadership. And, as the founders imprinted their wisdom and character on their generation of institutions, the Assembly will be imprinted with our own wisdom and character. In a generation or two the Assembly will have taken its place as a great American institution. It will become a vital check and balance that everyone depends upon in fateful moments.

In our system there has always been a cadence to the functions of governing. In the past, the executive office has been weak, and then strong, only to grow weak again. On occasion the courts have taken the lead. The legislature has increased and declined in its effectiveness.

And through it all, there was always the opposition, playing the checks and balances to head off the worst mistakes.

The character of the Assembly will be its own. It will be different enough to not be swept along with the trends of the Senate and the House of Representatives. It will take an autonomous place in our government, a pluralistic influence, cautioning and moderating the rest of the congress. Sometimes it will assume the lead. When electoral politics has the Senate and the House gridlocked, it will be the Tribunes who offer the spark to get things moving again.

Through all the years of our posterity, the Assembly will be there, one more instrument of self-governing for the common person—or the beleaguered opposition—to resort to in those fateful moments.

> (Paragraph 10.) "The Assembly shall not be privileged to secret matters of national security."

This is an appropriate limit on the duties of the Assembly. This paragraph also sets the stage for the unwritten rule the Tribunes should abide by: the Assembly should avoid interjecting itself into international affairs.

The Senate and the House of Representatives, along with the Executive, were established and constituted specifically to handle our outward interactions. They are the people's choice. They are long term. The Executive, edified by the Congress, is still our best hope for a wise and prudent foreign policy.

The Assembly should not meddle in those issues unless a terrible need arises.

> (Paragraph 11.) "Every article approved by the Assembly is entitled to a timely vote by the United States Senate and the House of Representatives."

This paragraph defends the rights of the Assembly. It also permits the fifty Americans to override the committee rules that have, heretofore, permitted one faction, even one person, to prevent the entire United States Congress from voting on articles of legislation.

This paragraph enables the Assembly to vote to pass any article of legislation, and thereby guarantee that the Senators and Representatives get an opportunity to vote it up or down in their own house.

> (Paragraph 12.) "Every article requiring the concurrence of congress shall be sent to the Assembly; any part approved by the Assembly may proceed and be made final; any part not approved by the Assembly shall be returned, together with objections, to the house in which it originated, who shall proceed to reconsider it."

This is an authority already inherent in a coequal house of congress. Once this Amendment is enacted nothing can be added to the Federal Law Statues and budgets without passing through the process described in paragraph 12 of this Amendment.

However, this authority is functionally identical to a line item veto. In the context of the legislative process it represents a line item approval. This is an ability to remove items from legislation, while still passing the more vital parts. This is going to be the most significant common act of the Assembly. It will also be the most hotly resented. It was, therefore, necessary to charter it explicitly in this amendment, so that it would be beyond question, and could not be revoked or circumvented by committee tricks or court rulings.

This authority shall rest with the Assembly from now on.

Many Americans are proponents of the Line Item Veto. It would permit the President to selectively veto, and thus remove, individual items from the legislation that he needs to sign for other reasons. The idea being that such an option would permit him to remove earmarked pet projects and political favors from must-sign bills, such as budgets and troop funding.

This authority was last tried under President Clinton. The United States Supreme Court ruled it unconstitutional.

A Line Item Veto is a game-changer. However, there is no will to grant it to the President. And perhaps there is wisdom in that. The thought of this tool in the hands of a partisan politician should give every American pause.

(Sidebar: Line Item Veto)

This amendment establishes what is effectively a Line Item Veto. This tool is sorely needed in this era of thousand-page super-omnibus bills. And during this time of high stakes partisanship it makes more sense to rest this authority with the fifty Americans, than with another elected official.

> (Paragraph 12, cont.) ". . . If two-thirds of that house vote to affirm then the article may proceed and be made final."

The meaning of this is thus: any article passed by the Senate and the House of Representatives requires the approval of the Assembly to be made final. The only exception is if, or when, two-thirds of the Senate and the House of Representatives have voted to pass the article. In that case it may proceed without the approval of the Assembly.

It is very unlikely that any party or faction will ever attain for itself a two-thirds majority in both houses. To overrule the Assembly will always require a bi-partisan arrangement. And by not joining the vote to override the Assembly, it is still the intransigence of the elected opposition that ultimately stops the legislation.

Any article that originates in, and is passed by, the Assembly (except resolutions made under paragraph 13 of this amendment) must be passed by more than fifty percent vote of the Senate and the House of Representatives before it may proceed to the President and be made final. If the President vetoes the article, the three houses may vote to override with two-thirds vote of affirmation in each house.

> (Paragraph 12, cont.) "If the Assembly makes no returns or objections within ten days of receipt (excepting Sundays) the article may proceed and be made final."

This is a constitutional guarantee that Americans will get ten days to read every controversial piece of legislation that the congress tries to pass. No more can the Senate and the House of Representatives rush through some bill, vote, and have it passed within hours.

Every article must be presented to the Assembly in its final form. The Assembly then has this constitutional right to sit still for ten days. The only exception to this rule is when two-thirds of the senate and the House have previously voted to pass the article. But such a majority can only be had for an emergency, or on a non-controversial bill of legislation. In all other cases we will have ten days.

There is no tiebreaker in the Assembly. The result of a tie is a non-resolution, like a hung jury, and the ten days counts down.

If the Assembly votes to object, then the article must be returned to the house in which it originated.

> (Paragraph 13.) "The Assembly is empowered to form commissions to investigate any United States government agency, official or employee for unconstitutional, unlawful or unethical acts of public authority; and for incompetent performance of duties"

Today in America the only agency that investigates the United States government is that same U.S. government. The political independence (and the independence from politics) of any part of that government is questionable.

The US Senate is unable to provide the quality of oversight that it once could. The Senators have not been appointed by the states' governments since 1913: the cynical and astute leaders in the fifty statehouses can no longer drive the agenda of the Senate. Appeasing the masses is the agenda now. The oversight of the federal government is subject to pure politics. The Senate no longer has any greater motivation or independence to police the federal apparatus than the House of Representatives.

The independence of the Assembly is established by its composition and by the autonomy given it by virtue of this amendment. The Tribunes do not face elections. They cannot be pressured or intimidated. Nor do they have a party to think of. They can take on the most popular leader. And the fifty ordinary Americans are perfectly capable of motivating investigations.

The politicians and their co-dependant factions will now be subject to investigations that they do not control.

> (Paragraph 13, cont.) ". . . and to investigate private persons and organizations who receive monies from the United States government (or otherwise act on behalf of United States Government agencies, officials or employees) for unconstitutional, unlawful or unethical actions . . ."

The Senate and the House of Representatives can investigate any person or any organization for any reason. As a full and coequal house of congress, the Assembly retains this authority. However, this paragraph establishes certain parochial authorities, and defines specifically what they are to be used for.

The gravity of this paragraph must not be overlooked. We are setting in motion a new institution. We have given it the authority to conduct investigations. It would be an omission if we did not provide inescapable boundaries to the scope of that authority.

We can trust the fifty Americans with the authority described and limited here.

We have to trust someone.

> (Paragraph 13, cont.) ". . . Upon two-thirds resolution the Assembly may compel the reform of any United States government agency that is not specifically established by the constitution of the United States; impeach any United States government official who has not been elected by the people; compel the Senate to hear articles of impeachment against persons holding elected office in the United States government; and suspend public business with any private person or organization pending congressional action."

With this authority the Assembly will be able to stop what should not be done. This is not absolutely binding. Anything that the Assembly does under this authority can be overruled by a two thirds vote of the House and Senate. It is a moderate check to add to our tools for reform.

But though it can be overruled, it may not be. Every Senator and Representative voting to overrule it will have to go on record as having done so. And while it is easy for a politician to do nothing, it is not so easy for an elected official to go to bat for an infamy.

We should establish and promote a spirit of zero tolerance for failure, malfeasance and lack of integrity in the employees of our government.

Zero tolerance means zero tolerance. Such conduct as we have recently seen should earn a person immediate dismissal from government service. Such an official or employee should be dismissed without ceremony or drama. Official misconduct should be viewed as "This is America. We do not have that here."

The ratification of this amendment will give us the opportunity to establish that spirit of accountability.

If we are going to stop the cynical plotting in Washington, we have to have a way to do it. That is precisely what this paragraph was designed to be.

Americans! This amendment is the correct measure of reform. It is restrained, yet adamant and enduring. This remedy is not an overkill. Nor is it a weak half-measure. The Assembly is an instrument of self-governing designed to enable We the People to remedy problems as they present themselves. The Assembly will be what is made of it by our future generations. All we have to do is establish it for them.

Americans! This amendment will actually make a difference. It will change the entire dynamic. This amendment is our doorway to the needful reforms. It is here now, at the right time, in the right form.

Americans! If you want real, systemic reform, as well as a new instrument of self-government, support this amendment.

PART II.

WHAT FOR?

Because our country is a totality, not a unity . . .

A place of our own, with a place of your own.

That was the promise of America. The little house back in the trees, the small business idea, the inclinations of you and your neighbors, each of these are as valid as the grandest common interest supported by almost every American. Folks did not come to this country to be conformed to a national standard of uniformity; nor was our government ever supposed to make war on our particularism. Society was supposed to be left to grow, develop, and express itself as it may.

This is the explanation. A radical prospect such as a constitutional amendment should not be explained exclusively by the problems that it would solve. If there is a deeper aspect to the cause, it should be included in the explanation. This part is called 'What For?' because it deals with the deeper aspect. And amid this inquiry is a basic description of one of the fundamental technical challenges present in any representative system: the balance between the common interests and the particular interests, between what matters to all of us, and what matters to each of us.

This is the deeper aspect to our cause: the never-ending conflict between the common interests and the particular interests. It is not what you think. Our situation is a fascinating paradox.

The renowned British political thinker Edmund Burke (1729-1797) once said of his native parliament:

> "The parliament is not a congress of ambassadors from different and hostile interests; which interests each must maintain as an agent and advocate against other agents and advocates; but parliament is a deliberative assembly of one nation, with one interest, that of the whole; where not local purposes nor prejudices ought to guide, but the general good resulting from the general reason of the whole."—Edmund Burke, November 3, 1774

There was a sound context to Mr. Burke's statement. And it fairly captures the nature of a parliamentary system. But it also permits me to introduce our system of legislature: The American Congress.

Ours *is* a congress of ambassadors from different and opposing interests. This is simply reality. Our legislative system is adversarial, just the same as our judicial system. It is official: the Congress of the United States is a clearinghouse for competing interests to be heard. In our system the President represents the whole nation, the Congress represents its parts.

The Interests

Taking a comprehensive view we can see that in any country there are common interests and particular interests. The two categories are not the same. The common interests are those that we all share. National security is a common interest. We may not agree on policy, but virtually everyone has an interest in securing our territory from foreign attack.

The particular interests are those interests that we do not all share. Anything that is a local interest is a particular interest. A local agriculture or industry is a particular interest. Sports, hobbies, political causes, and business regulatory needs are also particular interests. Particular interests are virtually anything that is not necessarily shared by all Americans, and yet might be affected by an act of government.

Today we are taught to think of particular interests as Special Interests. We have learned to resent the money they introduce into our political process. Moreover, we are conditioned to regard any interest that is particular as absolutely inferior to the common interest, and therefore due almost no consideration by the government that we share in common.

But particular interests are legitimate. The country is made up of particular interests. Almost every issue is a particular interest, and the government, which we all share, is affecting each of them. If the common government were only affecting the common interests, then only the common interests would need representation.

But this is not the case.

It never has been the case.

The men who founded the American government knew this. The system that they founded granted a very strong standing to particular interests. And it was agreed upon, transparent, and official. It was not based on money. These men knew that the USA would be a vast country, full of very diverse economic, political, and social interests. They knew that the USA could not be governed as a unitary whole, predicated on common interests. This is the reason that many of the founders insisted on a radically federal structure to the new system. It is also the reason that the system was designed around mixed legislative representation: a legislature with two separate and distinct voting bodies, both required for any act: the bi-cameral legislature.

This country grew and prospered in accordance with that system for 170 years. But then it was changed, and the changes altered the character of our growth. The issue is worth learning and thinking about. These changes explain much of the misgoverning that we are experiencing today.

TWO APPROACHES

Back in the 18th century the modern forms of representative government had not yet been tried. The conventional wisdom of the day held that a democratic form of government was only suited to small, homogenous communities, living within a modest extent of territory. This wisdom was founded on reason and on the experiences of the classical era city-states. It had been seen that democracy and democratic institutions heavily favor the interests shared by the most people: the common interests. It is all in the numbers; the common interests have more voting constituents than any particular interest. A community with a very narrow scope of interests fared best under a democratic government.

Democratic governments, legislatures, and any other voting body tend to be highly centralizing. The particular interests do not fare well. Hence, it was thought, feared, that a democratic government would prove catastrophic for the particular interests in something so large and diverse as a nation state.

But the political thought in The West was trending towards representative government. Many of the reformers of the 18th century were convinced that a workable representative system, with a strong democratic aspect, could be applied to the nation states of Europe and to the colonies abroad.

The strategies used to achieve this can be divided into two distinct approaches, which are rooted in radically different underlying philosophies. The fans of the French Enlightenment pursued a policy of unity and embraced the centralizing tendencies of the democratic legislature. This strategy is best represented in the parliamentary democracies of Continental Europe. It begins with the assumption that the sometimes dire necessities faced by the whole would inspire the lawmakers to always consider the wellbeing of the parts.

The parliamentary governments of Europe also went beyond this faith in goodwill and began to establish cabinet-level bureaus, or 'ministries', to represent and advocate for various classes of particular interests to the government. These ministries not only framed the regulation of the private interests, but also represented the needs of these interests before the parliament. This was how the parliamentary systems accounted for the needs of the particular interests in day-to-day affairs. The systems informed by this strategy have been marked by tremendous upheavals and often they fail to honor the potential of the people whom they are representing. Their history is easily accessible to study. The reader can form his or her own opinion.

In America, the approach was different. The proponents of the constitutionalism of James Harrington (1611-1677) and John Locke (1632-1704) recognized the value of the particular interests and established three principles to preserve them. The founders of the American system limited the role of all central authority; they chartered safeguards to preserve local authority; and they broke the government into three branches and split the legislature into two, distinct voting bodies: the bi-cameral legislature. Each of these was conceived to preserve the individual and his particular interests against infringement by the central authority.

These three factors are vital to our approach to government. But among them, the least appreciated is certainly the bi-cameral legislature. The internal balance of the legislative process was the fulcrum point for the particular interests of the country. This balance was defined by the differences in the legal construction of the offices within each house of the legislature. The house and Senate were set up to have distinct inclinations, which would serve to check on one another within the legislative process. And both had political ties to the particular interests.

The design of a representative office will determine the interests that it will serve. The crucial design factor is how the office is filled. The person who is holding the office must pass this gate. This passage will determine who gets to hold the office. In offices filled by elections and open to incumbencies of multiple terms, the person who would attain or re-attain the office is also bound to the constituents who vote to elect him.

Despite every other factor, the legal construction of the office will always be the greatest influence on the performance of the office and what interests it tends to serve.

The technical challenges in balancing representation are completely one-sided. The common interests are easy to represent. A free and open popular election will naturally favor the interests shared by the most people: the common interests. The loudest and most vociferous champion of the common interest, or the common good, or of unity, will win again and again. Or, if a more reserved character occupies the office, he will simply feel obligated to serve the common weal. The numbers of his constituents registering support for the common interests will confirm his feelings. An office filled by a popular election can be considered an office belonging to the common interests of the voters whom it represents.

Representing the particular interests is where the problems can arise. Things get a little dicey when official authority is unbound from the common interests. In most cases this requires a gamble on goodwill and maturity. But with a little wisdom and foresight a good system of representing particular interests can be devised. Such a system formerly existed in the USA.

Federalism And The American Senatorial System

The interlocking relationship between the United States Senate and the Senate-Chambers of each state was the technical means that provided legitimate, transparent, and agreed upon representation to the particular interests of this country. And an ingenious system it was.

In the beginning, the United States Senators were appointed, not elected. This factor alone enabled the US Senate to safeguard small, minority and particular interests better than a representative who must face voters in a popular election. This is one of the paradoxes of the democratic governing: freedom from democratic responsibility is freedom to protect the minority. But the appointment process was also configured to bind the US Senator to particular interests of his state, as well as to the interests that were shared in common. It was the legislature of each state that chose and confirmed two citizens of the state to serve as members of the United States Senate. Both chambers of the legislature of the state government were required to affirm the choice. Therefore, the United States Senators were bound to the interests represented in each chamber of the legislature of their state. They were also driven to fulfill their duties of oversight by the leaders of their state, rather than just the people.

The governments of each state are modeled after the federal system. Each state has an executive branch, a judicial branch, and a legislative branch. The legislature of each state was modeled after the United States Congress. Each state legislature includes two distinct chambers (except Nebraska, which has only one), and a majority vote in each is required to pass any binding legislation.

The house-chamber (or the Assembly, in some states) of each state was configured to represent the common interests of the state. Each office in the house-chamber was, and is, filled by a popular election. And each office is supposed to represent almost exactly the same number of constituents. The house-chamber is supposed to be equal representation upon the one-man, one-vote principle. The house-chamber is a pure representative democracy; the common interests reign supreme under these conditions.

The senate-chamber of each state was left to the state itself to design. This latitude permitted the states to configure the senate-chamber to best represent the particular interests of the state. This most often took form in the geographical delimitations of the state-senate districts. The state senators were still elected by popular vote. But the districts were drawn to enclose only a very homogenous community of interest. In other words, one senator would represent one community, with one major particular interest. Each state senator was elected by the most homogenous community possible, the type of community that even the pessimists believed could be served by a democratic election.

This was the original solution to check the centralizing tendencies of democratic governing. The government was democratic, but representation was divided up and allotted to individual offices representing cohesive and coherent communities. However, each community of interest had a different sized population. This factor required that one senator might represent fewer voters than another senator in the same chamber. This was what most distinguished the state senate-chamber from the house-chamber: the senate-chamber was not a place of equal representation. Each senator still had an equal vote in the proceedings of the senate-chamber; therefore, the constituents of a state senator representing fewer voters had a greater influence, per person, than the constituents of a state senator who represents more voters. Under these conditions a nation of heterogeneous interests formed and knit together as one common country under a common government.

This is not one-man, one-vote. But it was not supposed to be. The leaders of those days had agreed that some disparity was tolerable, indeed necessary, in the senate-chamber in order to more effectively represent the parts of the state.

This system served for the first 170 years of our history.

Sidebar: (The State Senate Chambers)

As our system was founded, the senate-chamber of state government was not required to be pure democratic representation. One state senator could represent fewer constituents while still retaining an equal vote in senate proceedings. The senate-chamber represented particular interest, via community locale. The house-chamber, as well as the executive, was supposed to represent the common interests.

The careful delineation of a community of interest guaranteed that the state senator knew exactly whom he was bound to represent. He did not have to juggle locales with competing or opposing interests. He was absolutely responsible to the one community. Each state senator served as a guardian of that community. Each had the inviolable status of a constitutional officer. Each knew his own role and therefore respected every other in their role. And even this constitutional state office was as responsible as any small-town mayor.

History has shown this role in action. The state senators were champions of their districts. They protected their people from infringement, whether it was driven by the next valley over, the state capitol, or the federal government. And they protected the interests in their districts. Any outside money, outside interest, even outside activist, first had to contend with a state senator: a constitutional officer chosen by the community to protect the interests of the community.

America grew up as a heterogeneous patchwork of distinct communities, not as a uniform wave of population. These communities were strongly independent. Local industries were owned locally. Economic opportunity was mostly homegrown. The important families typically went back to the origin of the settlement. Everyone who was somebody knew everyone else who was somebody. America was populated organically, by coherent, cohesive communities. And though we are a young country, we had established a stable, durable model of civilization.

The representation of the particular interests in the senate-chambers of the states, and the role that they had in choosing United States Senators, was intrinsic to the growth and integrity of these communities.

THE 17TH AMENDMENT AND BAKER V CARR

During the twentieth-century the technical construction of the United States Senate and the Senate-Chamber of each state was altered. The interlocking relationship among them was abolished and utterly eliminated. The 17th Amendment, followed by a Supreme Court ruling known as Baker v Carr, essentially eliminated the bi-cameral legislative representation and the interlocking relationship between the states and the federal government. Together, these two maneuvers eliminated every form of representation devised to serve the particular interests of the country.

The construction of the United States Senate was altered: In 1913 the 17th Amendment was enacted. It required, for the first time, that United States Senators be elected by a statewide popular vote. A popular election always favors the interests shared by the most people: the common interests, or those big enough to register as such. The 17th Amendment unbound the two US Senators of each state from the diverse parts of their state and made them into another instrument of the common interests.

Then, in 1962, the construction of the senate-chamber of each state was altered subsequent to a Supreme Court ruling known as Baker v. Carr. The case began in Tennessee, where neither chamber of the state legislature was observing the one-man, one-vote imperative. The Tennessee lawmakers were intransigent; efforts in the state to restore one-man, one-vote in the house-chamber had failed for more than a generation. The situation was not confined to a harmless abstract, as it might have been; the skewed character of the legislature was openly used to maintain unwholesome public policy, including institutionalized racial prejudice, among other things.

The situation reached the United States Supreme Court in the case of Baker v Carr. Formerly, the federal courts had held that state elections law was a states rights issue. In Baker v Carr, however, the court held that democratic representation was an incorporated civil right and therefore state elections law could be redressed in the federal courts.

Baker v Carr enabled the federal courts to rule on every state elections issue. It was soon evident that equal representation would have to reign throughout the land. It was no longer possible for the states to configure their senate-chamber to represent diverse particular interests. The feds had revoked that latitude. Beginning in 1964 every legislature in the country had to be filled by popular elections, strictly observing the one-man, one-vote imperative. This included the house-chamber and the senate-chamber of each state. The bi-cameral legislature was stricken. Without bi-cameral representation the balance of legitimate, transparent and agreed upon representation was tilted significantly, perhaps decisively, toward the common interests. The one-two punch of the 17th Amendment and Baker v Carr strongly shifted the balance of influence away from the parts and toward the whole. The effects are sometimes paradoxical. But much of the type of misgoverning we are experiencing today can be shown to be a result of this imbalance. This is the reality of the situation that we are facing.

The character of our government was hugely upset by these changes. This condition begs for a remedy.

A Word on Gerrymandering

Today, we typically regard the shapes and sizes of our representative districts as incidental. On top of that, we have learned to resent efforts to enclose specific voting interests into a single district. The folks who earn their living talking about political issues have convinced many that non-random shapes on the district map must be the result of cynical partisanship. They condemn any effort to enclose a homogenous community of interest within one special district. They call this a 'safe seat' for the party that tends to represent that interest; and they consider the practice responsible for the extremely long incumbencies we have these days.

The only defense that we commonly hear is that both parties get a hand in the practice, and therefore it is only another matter of contention that must be left to the free play of democratic forces.

In reality this issue observes many factors and is multifarious in its implications. We should consider, as much as possible, the entirety of this issue before resolving upon an opinion about it.

The first thing to consider is our present topic: a community of interest ought to have representation of its own. If, for any reason, a single representative is responsible for multiple interests, those interests will receive poorer representation. If these interests are competitive, opposing, or hostile, the representation will be worse still. One office cannot serve two masters.

A district badly divided by interest is almost a place without representation. The representative is compromised. Literally: he is compromised by having to represent opposing interests. He will have to serve cautiously. He cannot afford the risks of the fearless and unbending advocacy that we often long for; he risks offending one of his constituent groups; or he may provoke some huge outfit somewhere that will inject money into the next election, tipping the precarious balance in his heterogeneous district. One misstep and he is out. He can no longer fearlessly serve any interest. Thus, he tends to stick to common nationwide concerns, and ideological abstracts. His real convictions are held in reserve. He will always be less active and less visible than a good representative of the district of homogenous interests. The representative of a divided district is practically bound to serve the common interests.

On the other hand, no district will ever be a truly homogenous community of interest. The closest ever is the district with one single, overriding interest that is so dominant that even opposing interests know that they have a stake in its wellbeing. The example that comes to mind is the interests of a timber industry, in a remote timber region. The smaller interests will know that timber is still what brings the money into the region. But a district this cohesive is anomalous. Virtually every district will enclose competing or opposing interests.

This reality presents its own problem. The district lines that produce a fearless and unbending advocate for the greater interest also produces a near total disregard for the lesser, opposing interest. The constituents of this lesser interest are, in effect, sequestered. They have no representation of their own. A conservative living in San Francisco will have no advocate to make a public showing on his behalf. His local congressman will flee from the association with his interests. The same is true for certain liberal viewpoints throughout most of the rest of the country.

More than thirty percent of Americans are sequestered in this manner. This represents another aspect of the imbalance that was aggravated by the 17th Amendment and, especially, by Baker v Carr.

The Consequences

One example stands alone in its ability to demonstrate the imbalance produced by Baker v Carr. That example is the distribution of our representation in this country, and in one state in particular.

Illinois is a medium-sized state, about the size of Denmark and Switzerland combined. Illinois is well populated, with a great diversity of economic interests spread throughout its several regions. The geographical territory of the state is divided into 102 counties.

Because of the ruling in Baker v Carr just one of those 102 counties gets to decide nearly half of every variety of representation for the entire state. Cook County, containing the city of Chicago, elects nearly half of the Illinois congressional delegation. The same one county casts nearly half of the state's votes for the United States Senate and the President of the United States. That one county casts half the votes in the race for governor, and elects half of the Illinois state representatives.

And because of Baker v Carr that same County also fills nearly half the seats in the Illinois state senate chamber. The implications are sobering. It is easy to imagine how different Illinois state policy would be if the diverse interests from around the state were not tied to the population center of Chicago. Similar differences in public policy would exist if the state senate were unhitched from the one-man, one-vote imperative that so favors urban density.

Imbalances are never good. The one side is able to behave badly while the other grows desperate. Policy suffers and discourse coarsens. The imbalance established by Baker v Carr is killing us. In every state, from coast to coast, Americans are experiencing the misgoverning that results from a genuine imbalance of influence. From Maine to Oregon and from California to Florida this imbalance is an issue.

This imbalance is the starting point for many of the other problems that we are facing. So much of what we know is going wrong is either the result of, or aggravated by, this issue.

The consequences of the 17th Amendment and Baker vs Carr are very familiar . . .

1. *Unaccountable Government.* The community with homogenous interests is able to hold its representative more positively accountable. This is a general rule: homogenous communities can more effectively resist unjust policies. It is also practical rule: homogenous groups swing hard and fast against unpopular policies. This is the reason it is said 'divide and command'—the coherence of a group is ever and always the ultimate check on government.

America has never been a unitary, homogenous, interest. However, this country has been, and still is in some measure, comprised of homogenous communities. The diversity of our country is the reason that the founders, who actually thought things through, set up so many different layers of representation: so that each structurally-cohesive community would have a representative that it could hold accountable.

2. *Money in politics.* The second most common result of these changes is the increase in the use of money to obtain consideration. History shows a sudden boom in lobbying activity immediately after the 17th Amendment and again after Baker v Carr. This should be no surprise. Particular interests have important concerns. But if the legitimate, transparent, and agreed upon means of being considered is no longer effective, these interests will find another way. In America this means budgeting significant financial resources for lobbying activities. As long as interests need to play the game that way, they will play the game that way. And the First Amendment guarantees their right to petition the government in this manner.

If we intend to reduce the role of money in our political process we first need to provide a legitimate avenue to receive consideration.

3. *Party Politics.* The next misfortune aggravated by these changes is the power of the two political parties. A person who is located in a district that is dominated by opposing interests will receive little consideration from the representative elected by their district. They are sequestered. Their only option is to throw in with the party that most closely represents their interests, no matter how poorly that works out for them. They can only hope the officials and personalities of the party will serve their needs, since the representative serving in their name is against them.

This is the primary reason ideology has displaced practicality in our discourse. The party does not represent the person directly, but rather represents an ideology that everyone is convinced will redound to their individual needs. Everything is elevated into abstracts. Every interest is translated upward into a few principles. Everyone participating in the movement is expected to agree with these principles. The movement then employs ideology-scholars and other sundry characters to translate these abstracts back down into the practical realm. The entire mass then moves ahead according to its daily translations.

The use of parochial abstracts to guide so much of our thinking can only cleave us apart. Promoting abstracts has the convenient advantage of seeming to always support the common interests. This might even be true, except that the abstract is only a version, or a vision, of the common good. It is never perfect in practical application. This favors the growth of divisions and is a factor in the growing intolerance of the partisans for their ideological counterparts. The polling data indicates that since the sixties the two mainstream political sides have become more suspicious and distrustful of one another.

Humans will always react to an imbalance. And nothing is so unbalanced as the imperative assigned to common interests and unity during our lifetime.

4. *Identity Politics and Group Factioning.* The same influence that empowers the ideological party machines also empowers the pressure groups. The numbers only construction strips the influence from the smaller and particular interests that have not formed a representative faction outside of the government. Representatives simply cannot side with them against the more popular causes. Hence, the numbers only representation pays very real political advantages to individuals who forsake or diminish their membership in our common identity in favor of some alternative identification represented by a well-organized faction.

5. *Spending and Overreach.* The rapid growth of government is also aggravated by this imbalance. A great deal of this growth comes on the heels of some mishap or crisis. Passions rise, the public is shaken up

and the agenda can be advanced. For a moment, at least, the crisis is a common interest. The federal senatorial structure had been designed with just this factor in mind. The United States Senators were appointed, and served long, six-year terms. Other than the courts, no part of the federal government was so able to hold out against groundswells of popular demand as the US Senate. The founders described this explicitly as a check to rule by crises.

In the states, it was known that their senate-chambers would also be more apt to hold out. Spending the public money is always 'justified' as a common interest. No one ever promotes some spending as a good way to show favor to some isolated part. It is true that the parts are actually what is requesting the spending, but that is only because the parts are real, while the whole is only a concept. It is the justification they use that matters: if any part were to ask for a huge contract in its own name, it would be scolded and impugned as greedy and undemocratic. Happily for the promoters of increased spending, the masses can usually be convinced that the increases in spending will eventually redound onto the common good.

A representative office or chamber that is configured to provide legitimate, transparent, and agreed upon representation to the parts will be more apt to resist the cause of increased spending. The office is representing a part via legitimate elections, rather than lobby money; thus he is representing the people who will be on the hook for the bill, but not necessarily the folks who benefit from the spending. This is the competition of particularism the founders knew would check many excesses. The legislation is real and immediate: each representative will judge if his little corner of the world will ever partake in the benefits it is supposed to confer. This factor alone guarantees that an officeholder with a specific constituency will always be restrained with the community chest. In addition to this, however, the representative is designated to a specific part: to one specific, identifiable community. He does not represent, nor can he claim to represent, the good of the whole. Neither is he anonymous. The holder of such an office is typically less bold in his requests for appropriations. Meanwhile, he is more apt to oppose spending that does not benefit the part he is representing. Representatives of distinct parts are usually a moderating influence.

These factors are no guarantee. But over time they do tend to add an element of restraint to the process.

6. *De-Industrialization.* Next we should take a moment to remember the vast scope of industry that we have lost since the Baker v Carr ruling. Particular interest has always meant economic interest. Economic is the primary form of 'particular interest' that is regularly impacted by the policies of a constitutional republic. Almost everyone realizes that government policy has contributed to the decline (and fall) of many of the American industrial concerns. What is perhaps less well known is how this has played-out.

To put it simply: many government policies began to favor the larger, nationwide business model over the established local and regional concern. Even a business that is huge in a region is small next to the nationwide concerns. Since most productive enterprises are rooted in a specific locale, they have fared poorly under the numbers only system that has ascended to primacy. To be clear: this is again a function of the centralizing effects of democratic elections, unchecked by any other legitimate form of representation. Without legitimate, transparent, and agreed upon representation that is tied to the particular interest, and also freed from the common interests, the only avenue left is money. The common interests, and those big enough to spend their way in, began to receive the most consideration.

These conditions have favored easily aligned classes of enterprise and huge international conglomerates. Public policy began to conform to a nationwide standard favoring the nationwide players. Chain stores and franchises replaced local independents. Corporations began to merge like never before. Ideologies, which are shared nationwide, began to play a greater role in policy. Information and financial services boomed, while factories and resource gathering went bust. Blue-collar careers were replaced by transient service jobs in the urban centers. It is a story that we all know. And no matter what else may divide us, each one of us lament these trends.

7. *The Stacked Deck.* The increased taxation, regulation, and legal liabilities that totally confound mom and pop are handled easily by corporate lawyers. Politicians like to pretend that the smaller, independent, business model is failing under its own natural disadvantages in a free market. But the market is anything but free.

Prior to reading this book many folks would have been given to a general conviction that much, if not most, of our problems are the result of too much influence by particular interests. That is, those special interests not pulling for the whole, but only for their part. Many will have resoundingly agreed with the quote from Edmund Burke. But the reality is that it is not too much, or too powerful of an influence by the parts. Rather, it is an imbalance in legitimate representation favoring the common interests at the expense of the particular interests. This is not to say that parts are not wielding influence, with their money or otherwise. This is only to say that having no legitimate means of representation for the parts is a treacherous condition. Now that it has been identified it can be studied by its practical effects, which are the trends I have just cited.

There is no valid system that does not respect its parts. A whole is only a confluence of parts. It lives and dies with its parts. All of the ruminating about setting aside one's particular interest to serve the 'whole' is only utopian vapors. The parts cannot be expected to forsake their interests. World history in the last century discredits that notion. We must not rush to blame 'parts' for our problems. Parts are legitimate. Moreover, it is parts, not the whole, that are being wrecked.

Our Remedy

The Third House and its movement were designed in this century, as a remedy to the problems that we face in this century. Representation by Random Lot is more apt to militate against the minor and major excesses that we need to restrain than a remedy designed generations ago. And the Assembly is not a gamble on good faith: it is a moderate influence, rather than a decisive one. Finally, Rep by Lot will not face the type of resistance a rollback movement would. This remedy is the right option at the right time.

The movement for a Third House is itself a powerful tool for affecting reform. The movement will begin to improve legislation almost immediately, long before the amendment is ratified, and even before it receives any official endorsement or sanction. The movement, as I have envisioned it, will not have to wait to see results.

The Third House of Congress, as I have so far described it, is only the flagship of what will become an extensive confederated movement to fight for the interests of locality. Just as the present state legislatures are models of the present United States Congress, the Third House will serve as a model for a third chamber in each state. The decision whether or not to establish a third chamber within a given state is the prerogative of the people of that state. There can be no doubt that greater or lesser efforts will be mounted in each of the fifty states. Each of these will be of local origin, under local control, and moved by local energy and resources. These efforts will be permitted to succeed or fail on their own independent merits. This ethical position not withstanding, we will still be part of the same overall movement, and altogether allied for the success of one and all.

This is our remedy to the present imbalance of official influence between the common interests and the particular interests: Geographical Representation by Random Lot. The federal Assembly will maintain one Tribune from each state. But the states shall establish as many offices of Tribune as may be needed, right up to one Tribune from each county. The local interests of our country will again have an official defender and a safeguard against encroachment by the more powerful nationwide concerns. When we have prevailed there will be many hundreds of Tribunes, holding constitutional state office and guarding the interests of their distinct communities. This entire composite structure will toe the mark on behalf of the local and particular interests of this country. And at the crux of its power and influence will be The Third House of Congress.

This is how our remedy will address the unfortunate conditions described in this part.

Senate Revanche?

I would not be surprised if this part has produced the conviction that our system was more competent before the 17th Amendment and Baker v Carr. Of course it was! The original structure was carefully thought out. The 17th Amendment and Baker v Carr were incidental and thoughtless. But these changes were still the result of certain factors already mentioned. They happened for a reason and undoing them will face a bitter contest.

To restore the system as it was founded would require a United States Constitutional Amendment to repeal the 17th Amendment, and to overrule Baker v Carr, freeing one chamber of each legislature from the one-man, one-vote imperative. This would prove a bitter fight. The 17th Amendment was enacted in response to gridlock in the states' legislature that had left some United States Senate seats vacant. Baker v Carr was a response to the misuse of the districting to curb the civil rights of African-Americans. These reasons will be cited by every faction defending the status quo.

In order to go back, we would have to convince a two-thirds majority in both of the houses of Congress, and a majority in three-fourths of the state legislatures to do the right thing.

The stakes are extremely high. These changes would completely alter the character of our government. In addition to the high stakes, such an effort is also an all-or-nothing game. A whole different set of interests would ascend to primacy. Nothing in any conceivable movement to restore the senatorial system would effect the legislation passed in the mean time, or effect any improvement in governing whatsoever. The efforts during this struggle will accomplish nothing. The entire effort would have to be carried on and inspired by the promise of what is supposed to result after it succeeded—a very troublesome prospect.

This is not, however, the last word on the subject.

A Natural Alliance

It would be no overkill if both movements were to succeed. For while the Third House is a vital tool for managing our bloated domestic policy, a restored United States Senate would bring serious muscle to the role of oversight and add much-needed maturity and gravity to US foreign policy. And a sensible construction of the state senate-chambers could begin to heal the dislocation and loss of capital that has plagued the countryside since Baker v Carr.

If the will exists to roll-back the 17th amendment and Baker v Carr, the existence and influence of the movement for Rep by Lot, and ultimately the support of the Assembly, will prove a vital ally to that cause. It will be much easier to repeal the 17th Amendment with the help of a Third House and a nationwide movement for Representation by Random Lot. Most of the same logic favoring the Third House also favors restoring the original structure of the senatorial system. Moreover, the structure of the Assembly guarantees that, more often than not, the Assembly will be well-disposed toward the restoration of the original roles of the Senate. And the movement for a Third House does not have to wait for total success, or even until it starts moving the politicians. The influence of the movement begins immediately, on our schedule, not on theirs.

The strategy we will use to enact the Third House of Congress is the topic of part III.

Part III.

WHAT IF?

If we build it, no one will stop us . . .

You are right!

Our government is not going to swallow this bitter remedy just because it needs to. And there is no way to candy-coat it.

This part describes how we will apply our remedy.

Our Hands

We will not wait for the authorities to sanction our move. We will build it ourselves. We will build a resplendent, stone Assemblyhouse with private money, on private initiative. We will make it worthy in every way to become a United States capitol building.

We will do this ourselves.

We will convene the Assembly ourselves. We will choose the Fifty Americans exactly according to our amendment. We will install this new Assembly within the new Assemblyhouse and with every resource for the tasks designated in the amendment.

This too we shall do ourselves.

We will step back. We in the movement will step back and grant the Fifty Americans the autonomy of their chartered position. From that day onward the Assembly will operate exactly as it would as the Third House of Congress. It will observe every clause of the amendment. The Assembly will function according to every purpose that we have given it. Nothing will be less than formal. The Fifty Americans will lead the institution exactly as Fifty Americans always will.

The Third House of Congress will come to life on that day.

We will stand back and observe. We will watch as the Third House grows and develops. We will chronicle and promote the work of the Assembly. We will make a record of the decisions carried by the Assembly, and we will stand that record in contrast to the incompetence, waste, and perfidy of the elected houses. Every American will be invited to see what the Assembly has supported and what it has opposed. Each person will be given two visions: our government as it is, without the amendment; or our government as it could be, with the amendment. With each passing month the proof of our concept will grow. The dichotomy will emerge. Each person will be able to choose, based upon empirical evidence.

The choice will be stark: *America with a Third House of Congress, or America without a Third House of Congress.*

We are going to make a spectacle. That spectacle will be a fully operational Third House of Congress, established in an appropriate building, equipped with every resource, and passing its judgment on every act of our government. This spectacle will be the prime mover of our cause. It will persist, in living real time. It will move and grow and endure for however long that it is necessary. It will not stagnate or fall into decline. It will always be there: an ever-available source of comment and analysis on the present Congress. Every single controversy will beg for the opinion of the fifty Americans. The worse the dysfunction in Congress, the more the public will demand our amendment.

Our vote falls short in many things. But our right to vote can force this: a specific, common cause for a national remedy.

We shall advance one step at a time. From the earliest days we will be pressing the states and the federal government for recognition in law. We will ask for law to regulate the operations and personnel of the Assembly. We will ask for rules and protocols giving recognition to the resolution of votes by the Assembly. As we gain support and allies, we shall achieve these goals. Some day in the future the Congress will routinely hear the work of the Assembly, and the Representatives and Senators will reference its resolutions.

Our cause will triumph on that day. The ratification of our amendment will be only a matter of time.

When our amendment is ratified as part of the United States Constitution, we will be finished. We will hand over all of the proprietary rights to everything that we have built and established. We will go home, leaving the Assembly to fulfill its duties.

This is how responsible reformers apply their remedy. And this is how good remedies brush aside the obstructions of the establishment and the status quo.

Security

The assets of the movement will be its security. The Assemblyhouse will become the icon of the cause. It will be constructed with singular style and grandeur, so that it will be an instant landmark. We will make it a building that cannot be forgotten. The ownership rights of this building will serve as the leverage to ensure that the amendment is ratified fully intact and that the Assembly that we have convened prior to ratification is the same Assembly that convenes and operates after the ratification.

We will hand over the property rights only if and when the adoption of our amendment is made, to the letter, and accompanied by the assumption, in continuity, of the exact operational model that we have built. This means: everything that we build and promote will be the actual institution that becomes the Third House of Congress. There will be no room for last-minute compromises or a new Assembly of the Chosen. No. The functioning model of the Assembly that we have made will seamlessly transition to become the official Third House of Congress, with the autonomy and authority described in the amendment that we have all supported. Only then will we be finished.

The property rights of the movement are the anchor-point around which our security turns. We will all have contributed to the movement. And before long, everyone who cares to know will have learned of our cause and our intentions. The Assemblyhouse will represent the support and the greater knowledge of our cause. Any attempt to lay hands on the landmark through unscrupulous means will provoke popular indignation. And popular indignation is the best defense, and the only real defense, such a movement can have. Our movement will have sound defenses. We will have legally-binding property rights to all that we build. And these shall be backed by popular recognition.

Those in power can always find some dirty trick to neutralize our movement. But our popular recognition will stand as a defense against any nefarious moves by the political opposition. Even the most powerful emperors have been forced to tolerate opponents when those opponents have enough favor with the people. This is our security. America has no emperors. The worst of our lot are demagogues and vote hounds. As long as we are advancing in the debate no elected leader will venture to betray the millions who support our cause. No one will confiscate our assets or move against our personnel. It will not happen because any elected leader and his party who acts thusly would face fierce public opprobrium.

If anyone believes that the authorities would act against us by other means, by violence or illicit measures, then that person believes that we have bigger problems than a lack of balanced representation. That person belongs to a revolutionary mindset. Our cause will fail to provide the remedy that such a person believes to be necessary.

We do not believe that the authorities will forsake law and order. We believe that much of the establishment will tolerate this remedy while it grows, and come to support it once it shows its potential. We believe that many of our elected leaders lament the dysfunction in our system, just as we do. We believe that they will protect us, if all else fails. We believe that our strategy can, and will, overcome the political resistance to reform that we all lament.

We believe that if we go forward with this, and build a Third House of Congress, no one will stop us.

EXHIBITION

In a sense, the enterprise that I have described is one monumental act of civil disobedience: arranging the remedy, and operating it ourselves, until it proves up and is made official. It is direct action, like civil disobedience. But it is not unlawful.

In this country there can be no law against it. The US constitution guarantees the liberty to follow this enterprise. We can build any building that we like. We can form any civic organization that we have designed. We can empanel fifty Americans by random lot. We can investigate our government and propose remedial action. We can write model legislation, just as the think tanks and industry lobbies do. The

Assembly can hold votes on every article before the House and Senate. The Assembly can vote on those articles of legislation that linger in Congress, but which are denied a vote. We can publish this work, and promote it in a thousand different ways.

All of this is legal. Moreover, this is our right, protected by the constitution that we have inherited.

The establishment will not approve. But our strategy is designed to win over even the leadership of our country. The establishment will grow into the conditions as they change. Things move fast these days. After one political cycle the forces of the establishment will no longer try to confound our work, but will instead factor it as a valid and genuine influence on the legislative process. Another cycle will see members of Congress referencing the Assembly as part of the legislative process. The merits of the Third House model will have justified this.

The Fifty Americans will be fair and just. We believed that before we came to believe in this remedy. The Tribunes will be popular. The work of the Assembly will resonate with the voters. The resolutions made by the Assembly will be a credible reference on every issue. Any elected leader, a Senator, even a President, will find it helpful to cite the position of the Assembly when doing so serves his or her interests.

Time is on our side. The politicians will cycle in and out of Washington. But the Third House will be a fixture. The current occupants of Washington will be the core of the opposition. But they will gradually be replaced. The newcomers, fresh from private life, will have a different view of the Third House. While we may meet vigorous opposition, time will only lessen it.

Our remedy will begin to take effect immediately. Nothing that we Americans have done since the founding has been as adamant as this cause. The very knowledge that We the People are starting this will give the politicians pause for thought. That alone will improve their behavior by some small degree. The DC insiders will see the turning tide and alter their conduct accordingly. The folks in power will adapt, or be voted out.

The existence of the Assembly will compound this effect. The fact that a Third House was even built will stand as a silent but powerful accusation against the present institutions. Every mention of the Third House will renew the accusation; and every time an American is disappointed in the performance of the government they will remember the question: would this have been averted by a Third House of Congress?

Instant Influence

Corrective action will soon be possible, well before the amendment has been ratified. The work of the Assembly will be noted. Its resolutions will carry influence. And then there will come a day when some concept devised by the Assembly will go on to pass through Congress and be made final. That day will represent our first clear-cut case of corrective action.

From there our role will grow quickly.

Confederated Reforms

Washington is not the only objective. Our cause is to improve our whole system. The cause is not only a Third House of Congress, but also Representation by Random Lot, in any place where it will effect an improvement. Our cause is a general upgrade in representation to better control government in the expanded role it has assumed during the last century.

In many states there is a need for a third chamber of legislature. Almost all Americans have interests that are not effectively represented. In some places the need is overwhelming. Vast regions are practically unrepresented. Some places are situated so that they have no influence on policy whatsoever. The folks living in these regions will be our unshakable allies; these communities and their ways of life are endangered by the current dysfunction. In many cases, they will be driven to extinction if representation is not restored soon. The people there know this.

Rep by Lot in the states will follow the model of the Third House. Volunteers from within the state will establish a movement to promote the remedy. Each movement will convene to study the conditions within the state and draft a model remedy that suits these conditions. Each movement will build, for its own state, an Assemblyhouse and will convene its Tribunes. Each state movement will progress independent of every other, at its own pace, and under its own leadership. The movement for each will be allowed to succeed or fail according to the dynamics within the state.

In local government Representation by Lot is also indicated. Where do we turn when some governing body has jumped the rails? How does an individual remedy his differences with a land management council, with a city government, or a state agency? How does he go about correcting a Children's Services Division, or a tight-knit police agency? Where do we turn? Currently we have to take it to court, and to the media. But going all the way to court is costly and can take years. The media and its process is not something anyone should have to depend on for a remedy.

All across the country, local governments are not serving the interests of the populations that they are supposed to serve. Many are infested with carpetbaggers, flush with out-of-state money, and intent on transforming the locale into their own ideological fiefdom. Some are hopelessly corrupted. This is too often the case with our school boards, county commissions, and especially our city governments. But each of these can be submitted to a new measure of control by an office of Tribune, filled by lot. Any governing body can be made to include an office of Tribune. Some cities might benefit from a Tribune from each neighborhood.

A Word On Local Representation

The local aspect of our cause is at least as important as our federal Assembly. The movement for representation by random lot is a movement for the legitimacy of community and locality in political affairs.

The supremacy of the common interests, and the use of abstracts to explain far-removed issues, has distracted our people from the local issues. The intellectual class has also focused on the common interests. The products of the nation's universities and think tanks are geared to issues of the common interest and national affairs. This combines with the popularity of cable or satellite television, national radio broadcasts, and syndicated publications to remove many local issues from the forefront of attention. Even most of the commercial advertisements we see, hear and read are tailored to a national audience and lack local flavor or content. The effect has been to elevate the national issues to a status far above the local. Many politically active individuals express more favor or disfavor about candidates from other states than about the representatives from their own location, whom they can vote for and talk to. They express more angst or enthusiasm about far-removed national issues than what is happening in their own district. The energy of the concern discharged on national issues would be better applied locally. The same amount of favor or disfavor directed at local issues could make a real difference in those local issues. National issues are of more gravity than local concerns, but civic engagement in local issues and elections is a vital means of effecting the national affairs.

The local governments were the part of our system that was supposed to provide real-time (between elections) guidance to the state and federal governments. The folks would meet at the neighborhood level and elect a ward captain, ombudsman or other local officer. He would speak to the city councilors, the mayor, and the chief of police on their behalf. These, in turn, had access to speak to the county sheriff, the state legislators and even the governor. And these state offices appointed the United States Senators and could speak directly to the US Representatives. This is how the intelligence on local and regional affairs manifested to reach Washington. A reliable stream of advice and advocacy fed upward through recognized official channels to reach the responsible persons.

This was the American Way. This was the way the system worked before everyone began relying on unofficial pressure groups and "direct action" to obtain consideration. The neglect of this system is the primary reason the ordinary majority-interests of every locale are not keeping pace with the special interests. It will require a huge investment of time and effort, but this process should be restored, along with anything else that is done. A good start is to begin asking our state and local officials if they understand this system and intend to make use of it if elected.

For the purposes of our cause, however, there is no reason we should not have a Tribune—a defender of the individual—inside of any governing body that has shown a pattern of disregard for the individual. And a Tribune can be more than a mediator or ombudsman, which many governments already have. A Tribune is a champion, an outsider, an ordinary person appointed by lot, serving a short term. They are there to help the individual, not just to smooth things over: their purview can be extended to policy reform, rather than just superficial redress of the specific instance.

In the local governments, the office of Tribune will be somewhat different than in the legislatures. A local Tribune will be more like the Tribunes of classical times. They will serve directly, as defenders of the people, rather than in a legislative capacity. The duties and powers of the local Tribunes will vary according to the needs of each place. But Tribunes everywhere will be ordinary people, from outside the government, chosen by Lot, whose task is to hear complaints and take remedial action.

Each locale belongs to the people who live there. In each place, the legal construction of the office of Tribune will be determined by the people of the locale and informed by the conditions in the locale. An office of Tribune can be chartered to serve the exact purposes that the locals think necessary. The charter may require that the person to be Tribune has been a life-long resident. It can require anything that does not violate the equal protection clause of the Fourteenth Amendment.

The office can be given considerable influence on affairs: a Tribune can be authorized to terminate employees (which should be subject to review, of course), or to convene the council and compel proceedings. These Tribunes can be given just about any role in the governing body. The people of the locale will decide.

Whatever is decided and carried should be left up to the free play of the local dynamics and not given pushes or shoves by out of town interests. This includes the statewide and nationwide movements for Rep by Lot. The local efforts can contribute to the state and national movements (especially in branding the cause of Rep by Lot), but the larger movements must not provide material support to the local efforts. We need to give back our locales to the folks who live there. The movement for Rep by Lot must always respect the primacy of locality.

The Sunset Clause

The icon of our movement, the massive stone Assemblyhouse, will serve as a monument to our cause. It shall be constructed with impressive galleries of the finest American stone. In this stone we will write our story, the purpose and motivations of our movement, and the entire chronicle that we have made. And here in this new capitol building, on the eve of our success, we shall record the names of each person who helped to make this happen. We will carve in the stone itself the names, birthdates, birthplaces, and contributions of every person who helps to make this happen. That means all of us, many millions, for certain.

We shall not fail to do this; it is the final, integral, consummate act of our movement. This is the step that concludes our movement. We will all go home, leaving the world a little better than we found it.

The Example We Set

This movement is adamant, but it is no revolution. We will represent ourselves. That is a certainty. But we are not tearing down any part of what we have inherited. We are doing what should have been done in response to the 17th Amendment and the New Deal, and what absolutely must be done in response to Baker v Carr. We are finally going to submit this ponderous government to an additional measure of control.

But this is no revolution. When we have prevailed we will go quietly. We will hand over title and deed to everything that we have built. With the amendment ratified, and the autonomy of the Assembly guaranteed, the United States Government will assume ownership of everything.

The success of our movement will be a historical occasion. It will be only the second time in our history that a merry band of patriots took matters into their own hands, commenced constructive work, and finally overcame all odds to enact a brilliant success. It will be proof of the concept, set forth so long ago: that We the People form the government, not the other way around. This proof should be sent forth with our posterity as a cherished lesson of the regenerative powers of self-government. And that is what we shall do.

This movement will serve as an example for reformers around the world. It will prove that thinking and wisdom can outmaneuver and finally checkmate an out of control establishment. It will show that private initiative is the wellspring for reform. This concept, never before known to the world, will one day be known throughout the world. This House, began and guided by private hands, will one day take its place among the highest stations of our government. This generation, so confounded by a system in disrepair, will suddenly act to put things right.

And this country, the experiment of self-government, will not be allowed to discredit itself.

PART IV.

THE MOVEMENT

Details and full disclosure . . .

Americans should know and believe that the barest trace of secrecy is powerful evidence of ill intent. At very least it indicates a flaw in the character of leadership. No deception should be tolerated: not secrecy, ambiguity, or obfuscation.

I have tried to cover every detail in this text. Moreover, I have endeavored to make every concept as clear as can be. I have written this book to serve as a charter for the movement that will follow. It will serve as a contract between those first volunteers who take the lead, and each of the supporters of the Third House movement: nothing more than what is written here will be attempted; and everything that is described here will be pushed through with the utmost vigor and determination.

No action will be taken in secret, or hidden in any way. Every action undertaken on behalf of the Third House or Rep by Lot shall be recorded and posted on a website. All of our financial records will be maintained by a certified public accountant, and shall be posted in their entirety. Every individual or business employed by the movement will be identified. Nothing will be confusing or inaccessible. And the movement and all of its assets will observe the rules of the Freedom of

Information Act, exactly as if the Assembly were already part of the government.

What follows is a detailed exposition of our strategic organization and the intentions and purposes it will serve.

The Third House Trust

The entirety of the movement will be placed in a legal trust describing the purposes and objectives of the movement. The Third House Trust will hold every asset in trust for the day when our amendment is finally enacted.

The Charter Service

Our cause is not in the organization we build. However, the Third House model that we build must be independent from its funding and promotional apparatus. The movement must retain the proprietary rights to the Assemblyhouse, and the other assets, until the amendment is ratified, as well as retaining a position capable of enforcing the guarantees that are laid out in this book. For these purposes, we propose a Charter Service of the Third House of Congress.

The Charter service should be structured so as to maintain the independence of the Assembly from its funding and promotional apparatus. That is the first priority, if our model is to function as a true model of official operations.

The Charter Service should be organized as a for-profit service company. It must be set up so that the fiduciary duties correspond with independent funding and promotion of the Third House model. As owner of the Charter Service, the Third House Trust will receive all of the "profits" posted by the Charter Service. But the leadership of the

Charter Service will remain independent, transparent, and motivated by the familiar fiduciary duties of a for-profit service company.

The Charter Service itself must not be partisan. It must not endorse candidates or policies. Its purpose is described in its articles of incorporation: to build and facilitate the model Third House of Congress. That is the service that it will market, promote, and provide. The employees of the Charter Service are not activists. They are employees. Their duties are to facilitate and promote the Third House model.

The Charter Service is not tax exempt and its service dues are not tax deductible. This condition avoids the restrictions and difficulties that come with tax exemptions. This policy was adopted for specific reasons. A for-profit entity retains more rigorous property rights and more flexibility in its employment of resources. The Charter Service will simply pay its taxes, as every other enterprise does. It all goes to the same place in the end.

The operations of the Third House must remain isolated from any irregular political influence. Therefore, the organization promoting and supporting the Assembly must be unreceptive to financial-political influences. A non-profit foundation is easily influenced, or even taken over, by political factions. The trustees are elected by the donors, and the most generous donors usually end up on the board and calling the shots. We want to avoid that. We intend for the Charter Service to be purely a mechanism, transparent and empty of any ulterior motives. We intend for it to be an independent service company, managed by professionals, and deaf to political-ideological voices from other factions, or from the Assembly itself.

A Popular Cause

No one is to have any greater influence by virtue of greater pecuniary contributions. We are building a new House of Congress. It must not depend on important benefactors to succeed. It must be one hundred percent autonomous, just as if it were already an official institution of the government. This simply must be, otherwise the model and its record will be meaningless.

The Charter Service will raise revenue by selling a monthly subscription service. Each month the subscribers will receive an in-depth progress report and suggestions for promotional activities that they can undertake on their own. Subscription dues will be the same for all, payable monthly, or yearly. This rate will remain the same throughout the duration of our efforts. The Charter Service will not accept overpayments or large donations. The movement will obtain enough subscribers to succeed in our cause without these favors.

It would be unwise for us to allow our funding to outpace our real support. This effort that we are undertaking will meet stiff resistance. We need to act wisely, or our work will come to nothing. The assets that we amass and the support that we accrue must grow together. The assets and the support are mutually defending factors in our strategy. The assets confirm and represent the support; the investment of support by so many Americans will protect the assets from unscrupulous advances by our opponents.

The movement for a Third House must be a popular movement. We do not seek to build up a monumental structure or to present ourselves with grand pageantry until we have the genuine popular support to justify doing so. We do not want to be another fraud and swindle movement with deep pockets and no genuine spirit.

Nor do we want to present a grand target until we have the popular recognition to protect and sustain it.

Our presence must not outpace our significance. We will not accept huge donations that would tempt us to project an illusion. It is better that we struggle hard for every dollar, and thereby gain living supporters and friends of the movement. It is better that we have to stay active and thereby spread awareness among those who join us, and those who do not. It is better that we leave to our supporters only active, engaged means of providing extraordinary support, and first among these is individual promotional initiatives. We want all of our supporters to be active and engaged. That is the only way to produce the legal and political security that we need to overcome the establishment.

This is also the only way that we can correctly succeed with finality, rather than creating a new wound in our nationality.

> **THE THIRD HOUSE TRUST SHALL:**
> a). Hold possession of every asset belonging to the Third House movement; hold ownership of every business entity, including the Charter Service; hold ownership of every property, including the Assemblyhouse; hold ownership of every item of intellectual property, including copyrights, licensing rights, patents, images and trademarks.

A trust is a legal instrument, not a possession. The legal descriptions of a trust are practically inviolable under US law. Assets placed in trust remain in trust. Everything that we build will be locked-in and doing its intended purposes from this point on. Even if the cause moves slowly, the movement and its influence will persist. Everything that was set up will go on doing all it can to ameliorate policy and advance the cause of our amendment. Even if it is arrested at an early stage it will continue to exist. It will always be there to improve the process.

If this generation fails and the cause falls into stagnation, a future generation, perhaps confronted with even worse conditions, will be able to pick up the standard and advance it toward success.

AUTONOMY

The Assembly must not be concerned with the cause of its own enactment. Such concern will taint the work that it does. The work of the Assembly must go on without regard to how it may affect the popularity of the cause. The Assembly must act as though the movement is finished, its amendment is already ratified, and its complete autonomy guaranteed. All concern for advancing the cause must remain with the Charter Service. The Charter Service will retain total authority and responsibility for the task of the movement.

This is an important element of our strategy. The Assembly and the Charter Service will remain absolutely independent of one another. The effort to promote the amendment will not be given any opportunity to taint the work (and the model demonstration) of the Assembly. The two will not be cooperating, collaborating, or working together in any way.

The professional and well-organized Charter Service will not do anything to influence the Assembly. The Charter Service will fund the Assembly with no strings attached. The funds will arrive exactly as if from the United States Treasury. If the Assembly acts rashly, making itself look bad and setting back the movement, so be it. Despite what some may say, we actually desire that foibles expose themselves for all to see.

The daylight between the Charter Service, the Assembly and the supporters of the movement will constitute a self-policing balance.

The Charter Service answers to the supporters. They pay to provide seamless and politically-neutral support. The Tribunes, as the focus of the movement, can always raise the alarm if this trust is compromised. And beyond this balance is the imperative need to impress the greater population with the integrity and justness of our cause.

(SIDEBAR; A New Model)

The movement will promote itself. No interviews will be granted. No candidates will be endorsed. And none of the elite will be asked to employ their resources to assist in our cause. If the media talks about us, it will do so among themselves. If a candidate endorses our cause it will be for his or her own reasons. And if some elite is out promoting us, it is because they have chosen to, not because we have campaigned for their support. And each member will contribute only the standard dues. If a member has valuable resources, and employs them in service of the Third House, it will be on their own initiative, and not in conjunction with the Charter Service.

Independence

A movement such as ours cannot rely on existing institutions to promote its brand. We have no way of knowing if the insiders and the power-elite will rally to our cause. And if they do, the question remains: should we trust them?

That is a good question. We should avoid having to ask it.

We will not rely on the established elite to promote our cause. We will not ask to use their forums or their clout for our purposes. If they talk for us, or against us, they will do so upon their own initiative, not upon our request.

Any support that we could gain with a presence among the mass media would not belong to the movement. That is a strategic weakness, which we cannot afford. A mass broadcast is useful in leveraging the population. But we are not trying to leverage anything. Our interest is in sound growth, founded on the merits of our cause and on the genuine and deep felt conviction among those who support our cause. If we were to use some pundit to boom our support we would be handing them the keys to our success; anything built up in a given forum can also be torn down in that same forum. We see this in politics often: a certain leader will become the darling of a show servicing some particular audience demographic. Their popularity soars. But then they lose favor with that host, are torn down and ruined on the same show that launched their fame. They wind up the most despised person among that audience demographic and beyond. We do not want to blast the Third House into millions of homes under the auspices of some few media outlets.

Keeping the established media at arms length will ensure that our cause is referenced for its merits, rather than by its associations. It will keep us from becoming identified with the idiosyncrasies of the individual personalities. Perhaps even more vital, it will conform the language of the references to our cause. The pundits and newsmen will reference the Third House impersonally. This will depict it as a permanent institution, as opposed to a portable phenomenon of enthusiastic personalities.

For these reasons, the Charter Service will scrupulously avoid the grandstanding tactics that are so popular today.

Good Fortune

Representation by Random Lot is a hopeful cause. It has great potential. This will be made manifest as time goes by. We will only be thwarted if we make unwise decisions. It is unwise to become dependent on specific advantages that certain people may offer.

Happily for us, we do not need to. Our goal is perfectly suited for person-to-person interactive promotion: we have a singular nationwide cause; it is not divisive or polemic; anyone may be persuaded; it is an appealing concept; it will attract whole communities, often the leading personalities of every circle.

We have a decade in which to build support without the risk of stagnation. Our task is monumental and filled with significant milestones; as the milestones give way the work of the Assembly will become significant. The perception of movement and advance will never cease.

The vital forces of motivated talent cannot be overestimated. Our strategy is talent-oriented. As a for-profit service company the Charter Service can pay by commission. We can field an unlimited number of promoters without endangering our finances. With appropriate safeguards we can employ our personnel unmanaged and unassigned. This will establish a competitive environment: the best promoters will rush to find untapped areas to employ their own creative campaigns. Everyone will use his or her own native talents to the maximum degree. At the same time every one of our promoters and supporters will be active in promoting the Third House amongst their neighbors and friends.

We have an excellent cause with milestones to pass and work to get done. We can retain a veritable army of highly motivated promoters and supporters. Time is on our side. We will succeed.

Proof Through Practice

The proposition of a constitutional amendment should not be taken lightly. One that will alter the way things get done in Washington is of great significance. Such a remedy must be demonstrated before it is made final. And since there is no precedent by which to judge, it should also be given every opportunity to expose its faults.

We will have to do this ourselves. The Assembly needs to start its trials at the earliest possible date. In this way we can begin to establish a record of how effective Representation by Random Lot can be. We have to make what at first seems radical into something known, trusted and even relied upon.

This is how responsible reformers apply their medicine.

The Charter Service will, therefore, establish an ad hoc Assembly at the earliest possible date. This first model will be appointed by a two-step drawing of lots, will meet online, and shall conduct the work of the Assembly as perfectly as these conditions permit. Thus we will begin to see where Representation by Random Lot stands in relation to the politicians on public policy.

This ad hoc Assembly will have little enough influence. But Americans just learning of our cause will be curious to see what the Tribunes have to say about specific issues. The record begun here, by this Assembly, will lay the foundations for all that is to come.

Our Responsibility

The next milestone is to establish a site and build the Assemblyhouse. Two criteria are fixed in advance. First, we should site our project in or near Washington DC. By 'near Washington' I am meaning within 25 miles of the capit0l. That is one day's trek on foot. Such a reference may sound quaint or even absurd in this day and age. But we must remember it is not just for this day and age we are working. Someday conditions may again favor closer proximity. We may end up siting the Assemblyhouse farther away. But 'one day's trek' is the standard that we hope to meet. Every additional mile will weigh heavily in any decision.

Siting the Assemblyhouse in Washington is good, if the opportunity presents itself. But outside of Washington is also good. As a matter of fact, we can site the Assemblyhouse exactly as it suits our needs; we need appropriate spaces for all of the business at hand. The Assemblyhouse must accommodate much of the staff, each of the Tribunes, and public forums sufficient to satisfy the purposes already set forth. Finding space for these facilities in Washington may prove problematic. Space is at a premium in any urban center, even more so in the capitol.

If we decide to site the Assemblyhouse outside of Washington it may be that we resolve to build more than the one structure and instead configure the site as a campus with sprawling grounds. We may decide to seclude the structure within a large parcel of land. These decisions will have to be made in due course. The supporters of the movement will have the final word.

In any event, no matter where we site the Assemblyhouse, the ground on which it sets will ultimately become the property of the United States government.

The second criterion is to restrict the design proposals to the traditional Greek Revival School, as it is the architecture of Representative Government. We must do this as a nod to all that we have inherited, which is far more than our tiny contribution. We must not build some fashionable structure that is supremely vogue at the moment, but which might someday seem only a curiosity, completely out of harmony with the dozens of other capitol buildings throughout the country. We can innovate. We do not have to construct a copy of some Ancient Wonder.

But the elegant symmetry and practical features of Greek Revival should guide our work.

Greek Revival School notwithstanding, we still have a great deal of latitude in our design. We have all seen conventional designs: The US Capitol, where the other two houses of congress meet; the Lincoln Memorial, looking like a modern day Parthenon; The Supreme Court, with its Roman Temple design; and The Jefferson Memorial, incorporating elements of the Pantheon in Rome. In addition to these we have the examples of the state capitols, each of which remained true to the same School. We will use these as inspiration for the design we choose.

The choice of the site will depend first upon what locations are available. The Charter Service will choose the best site. The supporters of the movement will be asked to approve the choice in a referendum. If the chosen site does not receive an approving vote of two-thirds, the process will reset and begin again.

The design of the Assemblyhouse will be decided in the same manner. The Charter Service will accept any and all design proposals, and shall commission and solicit proposals from individuals and firms. The Charter Service will select the best design and the supporters will approve the choice by referendum.

This will permit the Third House movement to engage outside parties in the process. Some or all of the fifty states governments may choose to provide input. Civic organizations other than our own may have something to offer. The federal government itself may provide significant advice we need to observe. No one thinks we will have that much stature by this point. But we may. We may very well enjoy extraordinary recognition from early on.

ACHITECTURE AND SOME CONSIDERATIONS

The Assemblyhouse is more than just a new capitol building. It is a material expression of our idea. The design of the Assemblyhouse must serve the purposes of the movement, as well as the function of the Assembly. The chosen design needs to be symbolic, as well as practical. The design must be one of those landmarks that can be known at first sight. It must be so singular as to be describable in just a sentence, or referenced so simply as scratching a few lines in the dust. The design must be such that its renown can become near universal, like the Great Pyramid or the Eiffel Tower. How we will do this is something we must work out together.

Beyond the renown, the design of the Assemblyhouse must speak in the voice of the cause that it represents. This cause is Representative Government. It is also Representation by Lot. Our voice says that any Whole is comprised of Parts. It says that each Part enjoys a standing equal to, but not surpassing, that of the Whole. It says that our country is a heterogeneous Totality, not a homogenous Unity. Our voice says that communities, not just the majority of haphazard groupings, deserve legitimate representation. It says that ordinary individuals comprise communities and are competent to represent their communities. Our voice says that we are ordinary Americans; we are fraternal with the public; we are open to the public; we are not able to be effective without the public; we invite correction. Our voice says that we have lost patience with the government and its unilateral direction; it says that we are taking the issue into our own hands; it says "help us do this, for all of us, and for those yet to come." Our voice says finally, that we respect the goodwill of all; that we are not acting against 'conspiracies' or 'malice', but in goodwill and only against error. It says that we are not a revolution, but a humble and harrowed band that respects the gravity of all that we undertake to do. It is possible to say these things with architectural design.

The design of the Assemblyhouse must impress this message on all who behold it, especially the Tribunes themselves. To the Tribunes who serve in the Assemblyhouse, the architecture must say "You are a statesman now. You are entrusted with duties and responsibilities, immeasurable in their scope and implications. Your conduct now concerns millions living and yet to live. You represent a great nation, as some very great men have done. You represent the parts of the nation; many are counting on you. You are a statesman; you must behave as befitting a statesman." This too can be said by the design we choose.

The design of the Assembly must signify this message as surely as the text of our amendment does. For example, it would not do to build a windowless temple or and immensely tall structure. Nor would it do to build a compound surmounted by crenellated walls. The design we choose needs to speak with the voice of the movement. It needs to be elegant and majestic. Most of all, it needs to be appropriate.

These are, of course, high aspirations. But we can do it. Once we are in motion the personalities and talents that will carry the movement will begin to emerge. The character and style of our supporters will come forth. No one is better suited to this task than we Americans. I would not bet against us.

A Challenging Proposition

Building the Assemblyhouse will present its own challenges. The costs will be stupendous. But we are a nationwide cause. We will inspire millions to support us. It is true that we will not accept more than the standard dues from each person. But we will accept direct volunteer assistance. We can expect to receive an abundance of professional service, experienced advice, and even genuine labor from our friends around the country.

This is a tradition in America. Many of the other landmarks in this country would not even exist but for the enthusiasm and voluntary civic spirit of our people. Mount Rushmore, and even the US Capitol building itself, are owed in part to individual initiative. In many cases, voluntary contributions are priceless for the quality and attention to detail that accompanies them. Our strict limitations on cash contributions will not prevent our success.

We are in this for the long run. We will simply schedule the construction to match our means.

The Third House Convention

When we have completed the Assemblyhouse it will be time to convene the Assembly in its new home. The opportunity that this ceremony presents will not be wasted. This day will be used to mark a milestone for our cause. The pageantry at this event will reflect its exact meaning: private persons coming forward to enact a remedy to a systemic dysfunction. Our supporters will gather in many places throughout the country to celebrate the achievement. The newly minted capitol building will host its maximum capacity.

At the Assemblyhouse we will conduct each of our firsts. We will engrave the first name in the first stone gallery. Each of the fifty Tribunes will be formally sworn in. The amendment will be read. The operational protocols will be read. Elected leaders from around the country will be invited to speak at the event. The Tribunes will be given the chance to speak. Our story will be recounted. Our intentions for the road ahead will be declared. We shall strive, in every way, to present a comprehensive picture of our movement and the spirit that moves it. We shall establish our brand, once and for all on this day.

At the symbolic moment, the Assembly shall convene with the opening prayer and observe sixty seconds of silence. This moment will mark the achievement and success of this cause: only the second time private Americans have taken the responsibility for a remedy into their own hands and prevailed. And we shall prevail; once the Assembly is established in the New Capitol Building it will only be a matter of time before resistance to our cause is exhausted.

This day will not be forgotten. The Third House Convention will be a beautiful moment in our nation's history.

COMMENCEMENT

From this day forward, the Assembly will operate exactly as is prescribed in the amendment. Every official protocol shall be observed. This stipulation does not depend on the level of official recognition that we have attained. We will model the operation to the exact standards of formality. We will do this whether the government notices or not.

The Third House will truly begin to live on this day.

From this day forward the greatest care shall be taken to promote a spirit and morale amongst the Tribunes. The individual chosen by Lot is now a United States Tribune. The gravity of this role must not fade from attention. The design of the Assemblyhouse, in conjunction with the operational protocols, will be configured to produce an atmosphere that bespeaks the gravity of the enterprise.

With the Assembly established, its work becomes the focus of our movement. Every formality will be observed:

1. The Assembly will read and vote on every bill, order, budget or resolution passed by the other houses of the United States Congress. The comments, objections, findings, minutes and voting results of the Assembly will be sent, under seal, to the Senate and the House of representatives, and to the President; and shall be published throughout the United States.
2. The Assembly will draft bills of legislation, orders, budgets and resolutions, and shall hold votes on same. Each article passed by the Assembly will be sent under seal to the Senate and the House of Representatives, and to the President, and shall be published throughout the United States.
3. The Assembly will investigate public agencies and private parties that receive public funds for unlawful, unethical, or unconstitutional use of public authority or money. The findings of the Assembly will be sent, together with formal recommendations, to the Senate, the House of Representatives, The President, and the applicable State or Federal Attorney General, and shall be published throughout the United States.
4. The Tribunes may undertake any other action that is authorized under the Third House Amendment when authorized by a resolution of the Assembly.

The most vital function of the movement is now to promote the work of the Assembly: the record of 'what could be'. Each act of the Assembly will have promotional value. Keeping the American public aware of this work is the primary task of the movement during this period.

5. The promoters who have proven to be the most effective from within the Charter Service will be professionalized for this task. The Charter Service will become a PR corps, for the purpose of inserting the Assembly and its work into every relevant issue. The question will always be 'what if?' or 'what could be . . .' if only the Third

House amendment were ratified. No national policy contention will be allowed to pass without the position of the Assembly registering somewhere in the discourse. Those who follow policy debates will soon have a clear view of the institution that we have built. Month after month the role of the Third House will be showcased. By this our cause shall be known.

6. All of this promotion must be kept absolutely separate from the Assembly. The Tribunes must not concern themselves with the passage of the amendment. The Assembly must function according to its intended purposes, without concern for public relations. The Charter Service and the Assembly will be absolutely unbound from one another. The Assembly will operate the Assmblyhouse and conduct the affairs of the Assembly. All promotional work and financial support will be conducted by the Charter Service. The Assembly will receive its budget from the Charter Service, with no strings attached. That will be the extent of the relationship between the two organizations.
7. Complete autonomy will reign. The Tribunes will not promote the amendment; The Charter Service will not try to influence the Assembly. The record of the Assembly during this phase will be as perfectly relevant as possible.

Proceeding By Merit

We have cessation protocols.

If the Assembly proves itself to be incompetent to its duties, the members and leaders will have the means to propose cessation. The Charter Service will always consider the question. Leadership will not be the final, deciding, factor in the decision to cease our cause. But a conscientious leadership must take its misgivings to the supporting members. If the members decide to withdraw support to the point that maintaining and advancing the cause is no longer possible, then the cessation protocols will be enacted.

Cessation will entail the liquidation of all of our assets. The proceeds will be remitted to the members who have supported the movement, in direct proportion to the duration of their support.

We do not intend to cease our cause. However, the protocols for doing so needed to be included in these pages.

Recognition In Law

It will not be long before the Assembly is a vital participant in public discourse. The system guarantees this: no party in a serious contention will ignore the potential of citing the Assembly when it agrees with them. The time will come to ask these part-time allies for recognition in official laws.

1. In the beginning, American law is a neutral factor. We can build our Assemblyhouse and operate the Assembly as we have designed. But the government has no need to respect our findings, or even to acknowledge our existence. In the beginning we will have no recognition by any institution of government.
2. It is up to us to change that. By approaching this systematically, we can gain official recognition. Our strategy is one of many steps. Each step comes after the last. The ratification of our amendment is simply a matter of moving the ball down the field, play by play.
3. From the first days, we will be pressing the states and the Congress to make laws recognizing the Assembly and its operations. From the very start, the Charter Service will be petitioning for the states themselves to conduct the drawings to appoint the Tribunes.

Some of the States may well grant our petition and appoint their own Tribune.

4. We will be seeking anti-corruption legislation from the states and the Congress. Until this is obtained we can tell the Tribunes not to accept gifts and we can expel Tribunes who are found to have done so; but we can make no consequences. It is not unreasonable to ask lawmakers to enact a civil or criminal penalty for a violation of trust. Such penalties exist under the laws that accommodate incorporation. This request will be granted at some point. The states that support us will move to regulate their Tribunes. Other states will follow for political reasons. Any such law will stand as official recognition of our cause.

5. The Congress will be pressed early and often to recognize the work of the Assembly. We shall ask that bills or resolutions approved by the Assembly be given a hearing in the Senate and the House of Representatives. We will ask for protocols that require the entry of the findings of the Assembly in the Congressional Record. If we do not achieve this in wholesale legislation, we can ask a friendly congressman to attach it to some super-omnibus spending bill.

6. The objective is to establish the entire Assembly, and its work, through binding or non-binding articles of legislation. To whatever extent we can achieve this, the Assembly will be legally recognized as the De Facto Third House of United States Congress.

7. The effort to establish recognition in law is the natural precursor to the ratification of our amendment. With the esteem that the Assembly will have with the public, many of these laws should be obtainable. We will proceed, step by step. But, no matter how much official recognition we receive; we will not stop before our amendment is ratified and we have obtained the full autonomy of a coequal house of congress.

NO COMPROMISE

We shall succeed on our own terms. The amendment will not even be submitted for a vote until we have built the Assemblyhouse and convened the first formal Assembly. Our cause is not simply to see a Third House of Congress come into existence. Rather, our Third House of Congress is our cause—our Amendment, our Assemblyhouse, our Protocols, our Spirit. Nothing less than this represents success to our movement.

We will not alter our amendment. We will fight any attempt to water-down or to beef-up our remedy. We do not want to enact a 'gesture'. Nor do we want to decisively shift any center of gravity in our system. We want to establish a seat at the table for ordinary Americans to address domestic governing issues.

The amendment that you see is the amendment that you get. It shall not be abridged. The remedy that it describes is the remedy that we will build. The remedy that we build will become the Third House of Congress. The fifty Americans will become The Fifty Americans. We shall not be deterred from this.

No part of the Assembly, its duties, its powers, or its protocols will be altered at ratification. The Assembly that we have empanelled will pass seamlessly from their status as employees of the Charter Service Corporation to become Tribunes employed by the United States Government. The characteristics, the spirit, and the material record of the Assembly will enter our government intact. The Assembly that you supported and helped to build will become the Third House of United States Congress. We shall not compromise.

We will fight any attempt to alter what we have made. This means we will really fight. We will make the necessary sacrifices. We will put our lives and fortunes on the line. We are prepared to protect this project by civil disobedience. Only those who are certain should support a constitutional amendment in the first place. But with the certainty comes the conviction that we are right. With that conviction comes the strength to oppose any effort to alter our remedy.

One Cause

When our amendment is ratified, on our terms, we shall finish engraving the names in the galleries and cheerfully hand over everything that we have made. The enactment of our amendment represents our summary success. Our cause will have triumphed and no further promotion will be needed. The personnel of the Charter Service will be decommissioned. The Charter Service will cease to exist; it will not linger on trying to remain relevant.

This will conclude our work. The contract outlined in these pages will be fulfilled, every obligation satisfied.

PART V

THE SUPPORT

"So, you would join this effort . . ."

We have come forward to rebalance our unbalanced system. We have come forward to install a form of representation that is distinct from the one-man, one-vote construction that has displaced all other forms throughout our government. Our cause will be called undemocratic. But we are not here to appease factions and group interests in politics. The factions whose advantage we would diminish will surely oppose us. They will use every tactic in modern politics. But we are in the right. We can push back from that footing. We can push for generations, if need be. And we can build the Third House and model it for everyone to see. The Third House itself will carry the movement.

Our purpose is to propose one specific remedy, and confront and overcome the opposition to that one remedy. This is how things get done in a free system: by confronting and overcoming opposition in the public forum, not necessarily by compromise.

A TEAM, NOT A UNITY

We now have a strategy to restore mixed representation in the USA. Our strategy requires a strong nationwide presence. But it does not require a majority. This is not electoral politics. We are not acting on or through the authorities. This is a popular cause. We are moving our people to move the government. One-in-twenty is all that we need. If one in twenty are moving, the government will move. Five percent. We can reach that easily if we each do own our part.

Each doing their own part is the key. We each must act for our own reasons. We each must move of our own accord, by our own initiative. We have to think for ourselves. This describes a team, not a unity, or a corps, or even a federation. A team is a living composition of independent parts. A team is one when one is needed, and many when many are needed. A team does not require unity, loyalty, or a leader, only a strategy and an objective. A team is resilient.

The great status quo, and all of its forces are not like a team: they are a hierarchical organization. They are elite, powerful, well established. They are secretive. Their strategy is manipulative. Their motives are hidden, obfuscated, or abstracted. Their masses are trained to loyalty. Their leaders work for money and power. They are the material expression of their idea: the group world, the coercive unity of collectives, and the collective, the Aristocracy of Pull behind closed doors, outside of official channels. They call themselves idealists, but the numbers only vision is a terrible vision: coercion, in our name, willing or unwilling. Theirs is a terrible vision: humans, the parts, as only uniform masses of numbers, fungible resources to first justify their actions, then coalesced to carry them out. All together they represent the current establishment.

Soon this monster will become aware that we cannot be co-opted. It will learn that the parts and the whole cannot enjoy the same station. And when it does, a new division will take shape, one that has nothing to do with partisanship. It will be the status quo against reform. It will be the entrenched interests against the correct and just vision. It will be a tsunami of wealth, power, and status against individuals armed only with a certainty of conscience.

This move we are making is decisive. Better representation is a game-changer. Correct representation will roll back the trends. It will remedy the alienation of powerlessness. It will help to prevent any further dislocation. This will take apart everything the ideology of unity has built: it will permit us to force corrections to policies that ruin parts of our country. It will ease the desperation that convinces folks to pledge their loyalty to abstracts and material interests that are not their own. Much of the energy will go out of what is artificial in our political struggles. Without the artificial strife our vision will be clearer.

This means that what we are trying to build will indeed be opposed with all of the drama depicted above. The group-world will not go quietly. It will fight with everything that it has.

But we are a team. If we all do our part, not one month shall pass without something to show. This part describes what we must do to make this happen.

With the advent of this cause our long defensive slide has ended. Ours is now the attack! The tables are turned. They are on the defensive, right where they should be.

Americans! The Spirit of '76 is on the march again! This is the beginning. We shall reach our five percent. And that five percent shall move our people to again move the world.

YOUR FIRST ROLE

So, you would join this effort . . .

Our first and most immediate purpose is to brand the cause of Rep by Lot and the Charter Service Corporation. Branding is familiarity. Familiarity is essential to deflect attacks, to prevent fraud, and to establish legitimacy. Our first job is to spread the word. Begin with the most remarkable individual that you know and work out from there. Talk with everyone you meet. Speak face to face. Answer questions. Make certain that each person receives good and true information. And be diligent in correcting any misconceptions that you may encounter. You can do this; first person contact will always produce a greater impression than hearsay.

To this end you may want to study the almost three thousand year history of representation by random lot in the West. In 'the cradle of democracy', Athens, Greece, democracy was Representation by Lot. The members of the *Athenian Assembly* were chosen by lot. Aristotle describes the valuable uses of representation by lot in his *Politics.* Representation by Lot has a well-established history from which to draw.

You can also look back on historical events to see how earlier reformers plied their medicine. You could look all the way back to the *Plebeian Succession* of 494 BC in Rome and its *Concilium Plebes*, as somewhat of a precedent to the cause you are now joining. This event was the origin of the *Comitia Tributa*, which was a mainstay of liberty in Rome for hundreds of years. We are not alone in our need of reform, or in the strategy we have chosen.

It is not your job to sell anything. You are not pitching subscriptions or insisting on support. Everyone is selling something; we do not want to be identified with pushy sales tactics. As a supporter and a member your first job is branding. We will employ professional promoters to sell subscriptions. The rest of us will just talk about the cause when it is natural to do so. We are building a Third House of Congress for a few dollars per month; every American who is inclined to support that will do so upon his or her own initiative.

A number of individuals have expressed disappointment and skepticism about the rigid cap on monetary contributions. But this is what makes us a team. This is a nationwide popular cause. It is one thing and one thing only: the ratification of our amendment. A hierarchy is not necessary, nor is it even desirable. Extraordinary initiative should be appreciated and supported. It should also be honored and respected. And it should never be liquidated in monetary donations. If an American wishes to give more, they should spend it themselves. They should make an advertisement of their own or establish a group under their lead. And we especially want our folks to support the Rep by Lot cause in their locale. Let us do this in the way this country was built. Representation by Random Lot is presented here for each person to choose or refuse. Those who choose to support this cause *own* this cause. It is theirs to advance by whatever means they resolve to use.

Monetary factors will not impose limitations on our efforts. The Charter Service will pay its promoters for performance, by commission. We have devised a model so that each promoter shall receive commission for each and every subscription resulting from their efforts. Funding issues are not the limiting factor of our promotional activities.

We are calling private initiative to contribute professional expertise and voluntary assistance to augment monetary support. We want everyone thinking and acting, not just giving. That is when a movement is truly afoot.

GUARANTEE

This team is not engaged in electoral politics. No one will endorse a candidate in our name. Nor shall anyone ask a supporter to vote in any certain way. We will not attempt to use electoral politics to influence Congressmen, Senators, or the President. This is a guarantee. The effort to establish a Third House of Congress shall remain separate from electoral politics.

Elections are off limits to the Charter Service and to anyone else acting in our name. Instead, we will influence public opinion as it relates to the Third House and nothing else. We will move our people to move our government.

This will prove more effective than electioneering. It is the key to our needing only a small percentage: electoral politics is hotly contested. Any association with its factions will turn that heat upon us and split the country in half, for or against our cause. Obtaining a constitutional amendment under those conditions can be problematic.

There are also compelling ethical reasons to adhere to this policy. First, we are building a new instrument of self-governing. One part of the government should not be influential in the composition of the others. Even the Charter Service, which is not part of the government, should abstain from this tactic. Second, Americans should not be encouraged to vote for candidates over a single issue. They should also not vote upon a single, specific, project. This is the United States of America. We have quite a number of weighty issues to manage. The Third House of Congress is a vital remedy. But it is not, and never will be, an all-displacing concern for the voters of this country. If the Third House movement misses an opportunity because of this scruple, that is an honor. If we are right in our cause, Rep by Lot is inevitable. We can wait another term. Third, electoral politics is a dirty business; it corrupts everything that it touches. If the Assembly is to be truly like a jury, it must not be compromised at all. And electoral politics compromises everything it touches; it is a huge racket. We cannot hope to engage in that game without compromising ourselves. Finally, we should not be so naïve, or arrogant, as to think that we can directly force this system to do anything. Enacting our amendment is not in the interests of the most powerful faction in the country: the establishment. In fact, the more powerful someone is, the more likely the Third House is not in his or her interests. Only the organic and sustained inertia of public opinion can overcome such resistance. And that requires genuine and well-deserved respect. The strife of electoral politics will not promote that.

The Third House must avoid becoming a partisan issue. We are building a jury; it must be non-partisan. The building of it must be non-partisan, as well. And this will permit members and voters from either party to support our amendment.

You may be assured that you will not be asked to vote in any particular way. Vote your interests, but tell the candidate that you support the Third House of Congress. You also may be assured that your support for the cause of our amendment will not contribute to opposing your chosen candidates for office, or opposing the interests you that support in any election.

(SIDEBAR; The Onus of Our Responsibility)

These limitations on our strategy may prolong our effort. But we must do this right. We are operating on our system. This is surgery. Do not take this task lightly. Our duty is first and always, to do this right, so that it will not leave behind the bitter resentments of barely-won victories.

A Contract

Every anticipated concern is addressed within these pages. This text may act as a contract of sorts. It will stand as the terms and conditions of your support. It will always be a reference for you, for the leadership of the movement, for the authorities, and for any opposition searching for a way to discredit our cause or the movement promoting it.

The leadership of the Charter Service is going to read these pages like a constitution. Everything that is prescribed here will be pushed through with the utmost determination; and nothing that is beyond the cause here stated will be tried. No exceptions.

Beyond Our Control

This movement will face factors over which the leadership can have no control. The most common of these will be the work of the Assembly itself. The Third House, and every institution of Rep by Lot, are pluralistic, representative bodies. And so they are. Your support is for their autonomy; we are not building a special-interest lobby. You are supporting a living, autonomous remedy to a systemic dysfunction. You will surely be disappointed on occasion. Your support should not be contingent upon the Assembly favoring your position in every instance. On occasions you should expect to be in opposition to the Assembly. Your continued support is your decision; only know that any institution designed to represent the parts of the totality will not always be on your side. Furthermore, it is our role to set an example for our statesmen by tolerating genuine pluralism.

When you find yourself at odds with the Assembly, set an example for all the future generations who will not need to decide whether or not to support the Third House. Make use of the open-access protocols to tell the Tribunes what you think. Or make use of the system in general: contact your Congressman or your Senator. Tell them you are opposed to the legislation that the Assembly has supported. The other two houses still hold all of the cards.

The fifty Americans may be outright wrong from time to time. You should factor this into your decision to support this remedy. The Assembly will make mistakes.

The stakes are high. I know that a bad bill of legislation can have significant costs. But if the measure of a just institution is that it make no errors, ever, then we would have to dispense with government altogether.

Another factor, over which we have no control, is the actions of the authorities. They are expected to keep their hands off of this movement, its assets, and its personnel. We will not break any laws. We will play fair. And we will not interfere in their business, except as it relates to the function of our amendment. The authorities, in turn, are expected to permit the free play of democratic forces: they must not obstruct our efforts to sway public opinion in favor of our cause. We expect them to also play fair.

This is the plan.

But we cannot guarantee that the authorities will respect our plan. Many of our opponents will be desperate to stop us. This is a desperate struggle. Make no mistakes about that. We do not know exactly how determined the establishment will be to maintain its unchecked supremacy. Just because we have been free for generations does not mean we will not have to fight and sacrifice for our cause.

The primary indication of bad-faith tactics will be the use of official authority to obstruct our cause. As long as our obstructers are using only public opinion against us, we can assume that it is business as usual. We will have to tolerate defamation and ad hominem attacks. These are part of the free play of democratic forces. But if we encounter unreasonable legal problems, we can take that to mean that the establishment is determined to stop us at all costs. If the opponents of reform test us and find weakness, instead of resolve, it will be provocative. We must be prepared to meet their challenges. Each one of our supporters must be prepared to confront and overcome such a challenge.

It will not do for our cause to be stopped in such a manner. If we fail for lack of merit, then that is as it should be. If we cannot overcome the activists and entrenched interests, that is unfortunate, but it only underscores some weakness in our cause. We can, and must, tolerate failing in this manner. What we cannot, and must not, tolerate is succumbing to nefarious tactics by our opponents.

If the authorities succeed in stopping us by illegitimate means, it will potentially represent a fatal blow to self-governing in America. If they destroy a legal and transparent nationwide popular movement through crooked tactics, it will signal a new era for the elites of this country. It would be better had we never even tried than that we go down in that manner.

We should not even start this if we will not make the sacrifices, should they become necessary. If this goes bad, we all will face a choice: sit it out at no personal cost, or stand up and contend, whatever the costs. There is no middle ground. This is not for the faint of heart. By supporting this movement you have shouldered a great responsibility. You have assumed responsibility for a certain remedy; you have accepted responsibility for seeing it succeed or fail by its merits. You must see it through.

And this is not generic rhetoric. If the establishment tries to break us by invalid means we must stand up, together.

This movement is not one of those lukewarm outfits that say you have to lead yourselves. If this movement is confronted by bad-faith and extraordinary measures, this movement will provide leadership. You will not be left to wonder what you can do for the cause. Nor will you be left not knowing how far you can go on behalf of the movement without alienating yourself and breaking up the allegiance. Confronted by bad-faith, the leadership of the Charter Service, (or whatever is left of it, as the case may be) will always provide strategic and tactical leadership, as well as a code of ethics of what is acceptable in allegiance with the cause. You will not be told to lead yourself; and you will always know your terms of allegiance.

If called upon you must participate in the civil and political chores necessary to secure our just rights. Factor this potential into your decision whether or not to support this cause: do not join if you will not fight.

Destiny Verses Fate

Be prepared for all of these things. Steel yourself against what may come. Prepare yourself for years of slow progress. Some of us may never see our success. But we are a team. We are right, and we shall prevail. Each one of us will be remembered for the part that we have played in building the new safeguard of self-governing. None who serve this cause shall be forgotten. Each name will be carved in the stone galleries of the Assemblyhouse. This *shall be done.* We will carve them deep into the load-bearing walls. The entire Assemblyhouse will have to be physically destroyed to wipe out this record.

It is said destiny is what comes from within, while fate is imposed from without. It is the question of our generation if we are to stand up and restore representation, as it should be, or if we are to sit idle and be overcome by the fate of all former civilizations.

This moment is critical. The stakes are that high.

Printed in the United States
By Bookmasters

Dinosaur Sleepover